THE DEAD YEARS

HOLOCAUST MEMOIRS

Joseph Schupack

Fully revised edition 2017
www.amsterdampublishers.com
© Mark Shupac and Joel Shupac
All Rights Reserved
ISBN 13: 978-9492371164
ISBN 10: 949-2371162

CONTENTS

In memory of my father, my mother, my sisters, my brother,
my child, my Hevra, all of my relatives, friends, acquaintances,
all Jewish fellow sufferers and brothers in faith
who died in the Holocaust.

Preface

I have always wanted to write down the experiences of my life. That I finally decided to do so after 40 years can only be attributed to the support of my wife and sons. Moreover, I have reached a certain age and I may not have that much time left.

I have often told my children about events in my life and the Holocaust. However, I have never been able to record chronologically the essential facts of my own life and those of my family, friends and acquaintances in different places and in other times. With this book I hope that I have at least partially succeeded. It was important to me to create a monument to the dead to whom I owe so much, especially the members of my cherished Hevra.

I have tried to truthfully record my experiences during those horrible years and to include names, places and dates so that my story may serve as the sworn testimony of an eyewitness for the prosecution.

The fact that our enemies and those who feel their own guilt or that of their fathers dare to deny Auschwitz or compare the Holocaust with some small war, obliges all those who survived the slaughter to describe the truth in as great detail as possible.

Joseph Schupack

1 - Before the War

The events of childhood are decisive. Pleasant memories keep us happy for a lifetime, whereas bad ones can never be forgotten.

My memories go back to the town of Radzyn-Podlaski, a small sleepy county seat between the rivers Bug and Vistula, in the center of Poland. I was born there in 1922, and lived there with my parents, two sisters and an older brother in a typical Jewish shtetl.

Radzyn was inhabited by approximately 5,000 Jews and about twice as many Poles. The town and its environs had seen some famous Jews, such as the Radzyner Rebbe, the head of a Chassidic dynasty, and Zionist leader Menachim Begin, later prime minister of Israel, born in the nearby town of Brest-Litovsk.

The Jews lived their own lives. The Hebrew Tarbut School, the big library, the youth's thirst for knowledge, and the activities of the different parties and organizations were the focus of Jewish life. Jews who had turned away from their religion seemed to seek out alternative strong ideologies, and so there were many of these organizations and movements, often with youth wings, ranging from the very orthodox to the completely secular and from the Zionist to the anti-Zionist. Some became Communists, although this was illegal in Poland and could result in arrest.

My small existence, like that of my friends, centered around my parents' home, the Hebrew School, and the Zionist youth organization of which the school was a part – Hashomer-Hatzair, a left-leaning, secular group that encouraged its members to make 'Aliyah' and emigrate to Palestine, at that time under the British Mandate. There in Radzyn, on the fertile ground of the Diaspora, we were nourished with love for Eretz-Israel. It was necessary to teach Zionism; we were born in Zionism and we grew up with it. The

Polish national holidays of May 3 and November 11 were only pro forma holidays for us; our holidays were Purim and Hanukah. The biblical prophets and Chaim Nachman Bialik were our poets. Negev, Judea and Galilee were our provinces. The pictures we drew as children always depicted the sun, palm trees and the Star of David. Our coins went into the Keren-Kayemeth piggy banks. We were always concerned about recent developments in Eretz-Israel.

I could speak and understand the Polish language, but it didn't come naturally. Like most Jews in Poland at that time, my siblings and I didn't attend Polish schools, and the family spoke Yiddish with each other at home. When we weren't speaking Yiddish, Hebrew – both the ancient language of the synagogue and the modern Hebrew (which was not that different) taught in the youth movement – became our common language.

Thus we lived our own lives. My family was not traditional in the strictest religious sense. We followed the main holidays and the Sabbath, but not the myriad of rules that dictated the lives of Orthodox Jews. Mainstream Orthodoxy didn't approve of the Zionist movement, but we were free to participate in it. I planned, when I finished school, to attend the agricultural school of Ben Shemen in Palestine. Early Zionists were encouraged to go to Palestine to cultivate the land, and by doing so become ever more connected to it. But things turned out differently. Even as a child I knew that being born and growing up in this town and in this country could only mean misfortune for a Jew. As Jews, we learned very early in life that most Polish children had ingested anti-Semitism along with their mothers' milk. For that reason, we had to learn at an early age to live with anti-Semitism.

I remember the terminology used by the Polish government at that time, calling Poland a major power in Central Europe. According to them, the founder and leader of the state, Marshall Józef Piłsudski, was a great general. Poland claimed colonies in Africa, just as

Germany was demanding more living space. In the Sejm, the lower house of the Polish Parliament, most of the discussions involved accusations against Jews. At the universities Jewish students were heckled and often attacked by Polish anti-Semites. It seemed it was the "in thing" in Polish society to be an anti-Semite.

Also unforgettable was the widespread lie among Polish children, and some adults, that Jesus had been a Pole and that the Jews had killed him. This often-heard accusation would make it sound as if the event had happened only yesterday and every Jew was implicated in the crime. Jews were still accused of using gentile blood in Passover rituals. For these reasons, we Jewish children were ridiculed with insulting songs, which I still cannot forget. Every Christmas and Easter the accusations were revived, with new insults and affronts, often further emphasized by breaking windows. Sometimes I felt that I had known from my earliest days in the cradle that there was no place in this country or city for young Jews of my upbringing, class and education.

At that time more than 3 million Jews lived in Poland. The daily life of this minority was characterized by poverty, cultural suppression, limited freedoms, economic boycots, persecution and vicious anti-Semitism. Poland was a country of economic misery, overwhelmed with the problems of rebuilding a state that had been divided for 150 years between Germany, Austria-Hungary and Russia, with substantial national minorities – problems which had only intensified since the 1914–1918 war. It was also a place of religious fanaticism, rooted in the Roman Catholicism which lay at the heart of Polish nationalism. The Jews were always used as scapegoats and found guilty of everything by parliament, press and Church. Polish anti-Semitism was a sentiment largely propagated by the ruling class, who thought they should equal or even surpass the Nazis' intense hatred of Jews. Ordinary people, managed and encouraged by these rulers, executed this hatred through various forms of persecution.

I remember one of the traditional outings from my Hebrew Tarbut school on the Jewish holiday of Lag-Ba'omer, to a forest several kilometers from town. With 250 students, we started out at 6 a.m. and marched to the woods, where we planned to stay until evening. The sun was shining as we played and sang. It was still early in the morning when three drunken Polish hoodlums suddenly appeared. They threatened our principal and the teachers with knives, and demanded that we leave the woods immediately. All attempts to placate them were in vain. They claimed that we made the woods smell of garlic and Jews, which was not to their liking. In any event, forests were not made for Jews. The situation became so tense that we were forced to leave.

Another time, I spent my summer vacation in the countryside with Hashomer-Hatzair, to which I had belonged since my early youth. This time trouble was avoided, as we lodged in barns and tents far away from Polish villages, and were always careful not to attract the attention of the Poles.

When Piłsudski died in May 1935, the Poles told us that our benevolent "grandfather" was dead and that bad times were coming. They were right: his death was a blow to the Jews. Soon thereafter, Polish anti-Semites, by order of the government, were standing at the doors of Jewish shops, prohibiting customers from entering. There were days when Jews did not dare to leave their houses. And there were pogroms organized against the Jews.

The threat of the pogrom was always present. I will never forget the sight of the Jewish neighborhood of Brest-Litovsk which I saw one day after a pogrom in 1935 or 1936. I was in this city eighty kilometers from Radyzn with my father, a salesman, who had business there. It was early evening; the streets and sidewalks were littered with broken glass, and feathers from torn pillows and bed linen were still flying around. The houses and shops of Jews – if they hadn't been demolished – were barred, boarded up and bolted. Not a single Jew was to be seen in the normally bustling Jewish streets.

This incident made a horrible and unforgettable impression on me, only twelve years old at the time.

In Radzyn, thousands of Poles from the cities and the countryside gathered every year at Pentecost for an anti-Semitic mass meeting of the rightist ND (National Democratic) Party. The gathering was organized by two well-known anti-Semites of this area, the senator and great landowner Prince Czetwertyński and his colleague, the Sejm delegate Józef Bakon. Discussions at the meetings were dominated by anti-Jewish sentiments. Among us Jews in the town there would always be a foreboding atmosphere of an imminent pogrom. The next day would dawn before we could breathe freely. Only a few windows were smashed in Jewish houses and other provocations occurred, but no pogrom.

Due to all of these circumstances, we matured very quickly. We were interested in everything that happened around us: in our home, schools, youth organization, sports, books, and also in conversations that we heard – sometimes without wanting to. Such talk usually dealt with anti-Jewish discrimination and with the libel that the Jews were to blame for everything that was bad. We had to defend ourselves continually against injustices and false charges of all kinds.

In the late 1930s the situation started to become even more tense. Boycotts and Jew-baiting intensified, sanctioned by official policy. It was risky for Jews to be seen in some streets, and traveling through a number of villages was especially dangerous. The Poles even built a concentration camp in Beresa-Kartuska; it housed mostly Communists, but anyone viewed by the state as a threat to security or social order might be detained there. It seemed that the famous Polish national pride had free rein at the expense of the Jewish minority, with most people happy to go along with the scapegoating of the Jews. Democracy was as foreign to the general population as it was to the ruling class.

Under such conditions, we lived in the hope of a better future. This hope gave us the courage and the strength to withstand the day-to-day humiliations; we regarded our situation as an unpleasant transition period in a hostile place. The Jews knew how to get along, relying on determination, patience and humor. Jewish cultural life was alive and flourishing in Poland like nowhere else, and we all participated.

There were only a few Jews who were willing to do without cultural or religious ties to Judaism in order to assimilate into Polish society. But even they did not succeed. Although they actually were not Jews anymore, they could not become Poles either. The ruling class of the country and the majority of the Polish people rejected any Jewish tender of friendship and loyalty. Instead they treated Jewish citizens as hostile outsiders who could be used as scapegoats. Literally anything that was bad or unsuccessful in the country – and a great deal was bad and did go wrong at that time – was attributed to the Jews.

In these circumstances, it was no wonder that many Jews were attracted by Zionist slogans, or were influenced by communist and socialist catch-words and became members of these political organizations. There was constant friction between the parties in order to win supporters and to prove that their respective ideology was the best. The agitators proclaimed their wonderful slogans – tailored to fit any situation and often peppered with "impressive" foreign words that they sometimes hardly understood themselves.

The Zionists limited themselves to helping the Jews; the communists, however, wanted to make the whole world happy. For this reason the former were able to realize their plans, whereas the others still find themselves today only where they were at that time.

We became preoccupied primarily with the frightening news from Germany which overshadowed everything else. We had an idea as to what awaited us from the Nazis, but we could not imagine the extent of the destruction that would follow. We wanted to flee, but found that all the gates had been closed. The seriousness of our situation was demonstrated to the world at the Evian Conference shortly before the war started, while Hitler was trying to put his anti-Jewish laws and measures into effect. At that time the Jews were able to leave Germany and Europe. Unfortunately, no country was willing to accept them. The first act of the ensuing Jewish tragedy actually took place at Evian in 1938.

After Kristallnacht, the annexation of Austria and the German entry into Czechoslovakia, we saw the invasion of Poland and the beginning of the War on September 1, 1939. Unrest spread throughout the country. Food and other basic items were hoarded and hidden, while the streets filled with soldiers. Wives and mothers cried for their recently recruited husbands and sons: Jews too began to be recruited to the military along with other Polish citizens. In the streets the number of refugees increased. Blackouts were ordered and people became confused and insecure. The chaos had begun. Sorrow and fear could be seen on the faces of the people.

We children saw all of this and knew that we too were expected to look sad. But we were not entirely unhappy. As an older child, it for a while was exciting to see the sudden changes: the monotonous routine of life in our small town was over, and we could not yet imagine what would happen later. We were impressed at how everything had changed at once. Nobody was really working, and everyone spoke with each other. We could even walk down streets which previously were unsafe for Jews. Soon one saw Polish soldiers in increasing disorder and elegant Polish officers with beautiful boots, capes and perfectly fitted uniforms. We children had our first amusing moment when officers carrying maps in leather pouches on their shoulders asked us the way to Rumania. Any ten year-old who had ever studied geography knew that Rumania was almost as far from our town as from Warsaw. Still, we enjoyed telling the soldiers to look at their own maps and convince themselves.

Soon we also became familiar with the German Stukas and Messerschmitts. The local Polish authorities ordered us to dig trenches on the edge of town in which we could seek protection from the German bombers. Two or three days after the war began, I had just finished digging a trench near our house, when suddenly I heard the drone of German aircraft. Instinctively I ran away from the ditch. Within a few minutes, several bombs fell into the same trench and the entire area was under machine-gun fire. In the town itself bombs also fell, houses were destroyed, people were injured and some were killed. After this incident, I had the feeling that my life had been miraculously spared. This time it was not difficult, but would it continue this way?

2 - The Russians Are Coming

In the meantime, confusion spread throughout the country. Soldiers, refugees, spies, crowded streets, the downed airplane at the edge of town, the pilots who bailed out and the big news: the Russians were invading Poland. Poland was divided again, and once more seemed to be lost. The only topic of the day was how and where the border between Russia and Germany, i.e., between the Russian and German armies, would be established. Would they go back to the old Curzon Line on the Bug River or would the border follow the Vistula River? Radzyn lies between the Bug and Vistula Rivers.

In the town, unrest, tension and excitement prevailed. There were heated discussions, particularly among our Jewish boys, since our futures were at stake. Hitler and Nazism or freedom under communism? Under the Nazis there was only oppression and slavery; on the other hand, we expected communism to be the complete liberation of all working and peace-loving people. All the idealistic slogans and phrases which were spoken and written about communism would now become reality. Our Zionist dreams had proved to be illusory and seemed to have been overtaken by historical events. Jews with a communist past, especially those who were imprisoned for small crimes like hanging red flags from the electrical cables in town, or putting up communist posters, believed that with the Russians the long-awaited day of liberation would come.

Soon news arrived that outposts of the Red Army had been seen in towns and villages nearby. Especially us Jews were ecstatic. The roads in and out of the town were, however, still crowded with divisions of the Polish Army: cavalry, infantry and artillery. There was constant movement in the streets. In the nearby woods and villages, the rest of the Polish Army was regrouping. On the edge of town some Russian trucks with soldiers of the Red Army appeared.

The local communists, with their red armbands, welcomed their Russian comrades. They received rifles from them and proceeded to take control of the town. All the dreams of the Red Revolution, it seemed, would come true within minutes. The great liberation had begun. The remaining police officers were stripped of their power and public offices were taken over. Enemies of communism and anti-Semites were quickly prosecuted and relieved of their duties. The majority of them, however, had already gone into hiding out of fear.

Many older Jews of the upper classes and the Zionists were more restrained. The majority, however, were glad to have witnessed that day – the day on which the promise of the Red Revolution would be fulfilled. The poor would become rich, the hungry satiated and the oppressed free. Their reaction was understandable in light of their difficult life among the Poles.

Things became more chaotic in the town. New military units arrived and then disappeared. Some soldiers deserted and dressed as civilians. Artillery fire could be heard from far away and nearby. The wearers of red armbands, most of them young and Jewish, were conspicuous as they raced back and forth on confiscated bicycles or in coaches drawn by fine horses.

I observed all this with respect and perhaps with some jealousy, too. I felt like someone who had bet on the wrong horse. After some consideration, I found an excuse in my lack of experience at age seventeen. I was also consoled by the recognition that I was pink, although it was clear that only true red was acceptable at the moment. To play an important part, I would have to have been older and redder. I regretted that.

Among the new rulers with the red armbands, I recognized Abraham Pinkus who was their leader. I knew him very well, since he worked at the town's power plant where I had recently found a job. I hoped to catch his eye, but he seemed too busy. He did not appear to see anyone and certainly not me. That was actually the big day (it was mid-September 1939) for Mr. Pinkus and his comrades – the day they made history. Whether or not it was their best day, I do not know.

The day was hardly over when the Russians on the edge of town moved their trucks eastwards and the world of Abraham Pinkus and his comrades fell apart completely. The Polish cavalry instantly appeared, accompanied by anti-Semites of all kinds who took over the city. Old scores were to be settled. With the Russians, the new communist leaders also left, using any available means of transportation for their trek eastwards. Those who had recently been imprisoned were set free. Many Jews hid once more. The new arrivals looted, shot and attacked Jews, and waged the war which they intended to fight against the Germans against us with their horses and sabers.

As a young and curious person, I always found myself in the middle of the action. After the recent turn of events, I managed to reach home (my parents' house) only with great effort and skill. From far away I could see that the door and shutters on the street side of the house were locked. No one heard me as I knocked and shouted. All of the neighboring homes were also shuttered. I quickly ran to the back door and was finally let in. Lying on the floor and under the beds, I found my family terrified. In the immediate proximity we could hear shooting and the banging of rifle butts on our door and shutters; some shots went through our wall. A few minutes later I heard Polish soldiers accompanied by a street gang banging at our back door – the same door through which I had just entered the house. Only one door led to our apartment, another three led to other Jewish families. From what we could hear, it was clear that they were looking for the communist leader who worked at the power plant, Abraham Pinkus. Because the street gang did not know exactly who they meant, they led the soldiers to our house, to me, since I also worked there. It was not difficult to kick the first door, leading to our neighbor's apartment, open. Innocently, our neighbor Sarah Kaweblum, a baker's wife, came to the door with a baby in her arms. The Polish soldiers fired immediately, shooting off her right hand before disappearing. For the next two years I saw that woman with only a stump for an arm almost every day. The bullets that hit her, meant for Abraham Pinkus, were in fact, because of a case of mistaken identity, intended for me. My heart ached every time I saw her. Thus my life had been spared a second time – once again by chance.

3 - The Germans Are Here

The Russians left, but the Germans marched into Radzyn. The new border was established along the River Bug. For several weeks this border was considered easy to cross. Those months were the honeymoon period of the Hitler-Stalin Pact. Among the Jewish population, especially the young people, a lively migration eastwards started to Brest-Litovsk, which was only about 80 kilometers from Radzyn.

Many, particularly older people, did not want to flee. They remembered the bitter misery of refugees during World War I and somehow found the courage to persevere. From their experiences during that war, they thought it would be possible to live with the Germans. However, with the different groups of Germans that passed through (we could hardly tell the difference between the various police units and the members of the Wehrmacht), the Jewish population soon felt the impact of the Nazis: violence, pillage, desecration of synagogues, hostage taking, forced labor, all of which were often supported by Polish anti-Semites. These acts were followed by periods in which we could live in relative calm. Optimists believed that each break was the end of our suffering, but pessimists believed the situation would worsen. The latter were right.

My own situation changed somewhat because, after the communist "king for a day" Abraham Pinkus disappeared, I was the only Jew left working at the plant. Unlike the Polish employees, I was able to communicate with the German soldiers, which made me an important person, a so-called "useful" Jew. Thus I could help my family and move about relatively freely. I also was able to save my father from occasional forced labor, which was painful and often dangerous. But soon, German-speaking migrants from the western part of Poland arrived and my future began to look bleak. Eventually

I succeeded in working exclusively for the German authorities so that I could partly maintain my privileges as a useful Jew.

When the German Wehrmacht marched in, the center of the town, which was inhabited only by Jews, was evacuated and fenced in with barbed wire. The houses were used as barracks for soldiers and the two big synagogues as stables. The same treatment was accorded the synagogue and yeshiva of the famous Rabbi of Radzyn. The furnishings of the synagogues had already been desecrated and demolished. Every new unit that marched into town seemed obligated to vandalize. After demanding contributions, seizing hostages and plundering Jewish stores, the German occupation troops made themselves at home and the German authorities further tightened the screws on us Jews. Theft, murder and forced labor in rain, snow and mud became part of the everyday routine. Instead of horses, Jews were harnessed to wagons loaded with coal and other goods. A favorite sadistic sport was cutting Jews' beards off with a knife or scissors, or setting them on fire. Many Jews with beards wore bandages on their faces, pretending to be wounded already. Every Jewish establishment and prayer house was desecrated as a matter of course.

A Judenrat was founded. In our city only one person could be chosen as the elder of the Jews: Herr David Lichtenstein. Rich, well respected, energetic and arrogant, he had the chutzpah to call everyone by their first names. He had all the traits one would expect in a Jewish elder. Thanks to his intelligence, he was sometimes able to tame the uniformed German sadists by means of kind words and expensive gifts, and to prevent them from dragging Jews off to work at any time, day or night. Still, life became more difficult with each new day.

I only had a few friends left, since most had fled to the Russians or were planning to do so as they realized that life under the Nazis was impossible. I had similar thoughts although my family was staying here. It was difficult for me to make up my mind. After all, I was barely seventeen years old and had never been separated from my family, except for vacations at the Hashomer-Hatzair summer camp, where I was in the company of 50 to 100 friends of the same age.

One day I saw how SS members herded up the well-respected and officially-appointed Rav – his name was Fein – along with other well-known, religious, bearded Jews at the bus stop in the center of town. They were ordered to bring their Torahs and to unroll them. They were forced to put on their tallits and tefilin and then to sing and dance on their Torahs. Their beards were cut off with knives and scissors or were set on fire. They were brutally tortured and beaten by the SS. As I witnessed it all with my own eyes, I decided to flee to the east immediately. Several cruel episodes of this kind occurred. As a consequence, our famous Rabbi Leiner lived in hiding with his Hasidic followers. Later he went to Wlodawa, a border town on the Bug, where he disguised himself as a shoemaker. As our situation deteriorated, his words of consolation and encouragement reached us. They gave us courage and new faith. He called upon the Jews to resist, and organize themselves in the woods. I do not know exactly how he died. He was probably denounced and then shot by the SS.

On November 5, 1939 I packed my knapsack, took my bicycle and headed east, in the direction of the Bug, which was about 80 kilometers from Radzyn. With the unnerving events of the last few days still fresh in my mind, I reached the border at Wlodawa after a few hours. In the evening I joined a group of people who were headed for the same destination. After paying smugglers, we – there were nine to ten of us – climbed into a small boat to cross the River Bug and proceeded to Brest-Litovsk. I carried my bicycle over my head. After 20 minutes we reached the opposite bank. It must have been around midnight and we had to hide again, tired, hungry and thirsty. After walking through the darkness I fell asleep somewhere. When I woke up in the morning, I noticed that I had slept in the mud close to a deserted summerhouse in Domaczewa near Brest-Litovsk.

My bicycle had disappeared. We saw Russian soldiers, and they saw us. It appeared to be a sort of silent understanding.

4 - With the Russians in Brest-Litovsk

In the evening of the next day, I arrived at Brest, a big city on the border which was occupied by the Russians. Unlike my hometown Radzyn where everything was dark either out of fear or as a way of not provoking the Germans, the streets and houses of Brest were more than well lit. Gigantic portraits of Marx, Lenin, Stalin and other heroes of that time were brightly illuminated, and people filled the streets with song and laughter. I was quite impressed – it was how I imagined freedom would be.

Very soon, however, I was confronted with the seriousness of the situation. The city was hopelessly flooded with refugees. It was almost impossible to find a place to sleep. I had little money and even less experience, being on my own for the first time in my life. I had neither relatives nor friends in Brest, with the exception of one friend who lived with his aunt. I stayed with him in their overcrowded house. We slept on tiny straw mattresses on the floor. I soon found out why the streets were so festively decorated and illuminated on my first evening in Brest. It was the eve of November 7, the 22nd anniversary of the Russian Revolution. On the morning of the big day there was a great deal going on in the streets: marching bands, military parades, music, singing and young people dancing. There were pictures and gigantic portraits of all the communist heroes. Of course Stalin's portrait was the biggest of all; big Stalin, bigger Stalin and even bigger Stalin. Some of the pictures were so large that they were hung from two beams which had to be carried by six people on either side.

Even I looked festive. I had brought my best clothes with me and was wearing them for this occasion. I had put on a pair of handsome boots which were perfect for the ceremony and felt comfortable and in good spirits. I admit that on that day I forgot about my Zionist attitude and all my troubles. The communists were right: Freedom for everyone! Why should one fight only for the Jewish and Zionist causes?

We Jewish boys discussed this subject for days and nights. Our opinions were always divided and we were never able to agree on the better and more just way. On that day, however, influenced by the euphoria and gala atmosphere, even I was willing to forget my previous views and to admit my errors: the communists were actually right.

With all my strength I fought my way into the parade in the hope of obtaining a place in the front, so that I could carry one of the oversized Stalin portraits. As a sort of reconciliation, I wanted to carry the picture myself, regardless of how large it was. I soon felt the heavy beam press against my shoulder. Periodically I glanced up at Stalin and saw him benevolently smiling down on me; I felt thankful and indebted to him.

At that time of year it was cold and rainy. The roads were muddy and my shoes were soon soaked. Cold and damp crept into my body and I became ever more miserable. Looking up, I thought that Stalin must have felt the same way; he seemed to become progressively more indignant. This human god seemed to enjoy the ignorance of the people.

Finally I asked myself why any human being should be a god and be served. I suddenly changed my attitude and let others carry him. I left angered at the demonstration and promised myself never to carry or serve any human god again. To this day I have lived up to this promise.

During my stay in Brest-Litovsk I met some of my best friends from school and Hashomer-Hatzair. We spent our time discussing old topics, new situations and admiring the Red Army. None of us were able to find a job. As a refugee one could only find temporary arrangements. The meaning of life was limited to enjoying freedom and admiring it along with those who liberated us. In the meantime our worries grew and our pockets were becoming empty, our shirts dirty and our feet wet – we were hungry and felt miserable. What to do? A few loyal communists either found important municipal jobs or left for the center of Russia. The others who stayed – they were the majority – did good business with Russian soldiers who were curious about any consumer goods they did not know.

Every day thousands of merchants gathered in the marketplace, the so-called Tolciok. The Russian soldiers had a lot of money and bought everything. There it was possible to sell two right or two left shoes of different sizes or even one shoe alone. The trade of nightgowns as evening gowns and brassieres flourished. Watches were particularly in demand. Even if a Russian soldier already had two watches – one on each wrist – he still purchased more and wore them one on top of the other. Alarm clocks were also sought after. They did not have to work as long as the alarm rang. The ticking could be simulated by the seller himself or by a friend standing nearby. It was the only place where literally anything could be bought and sold. Laughter was constantly heard; one laughed at the other, the sellers laughed at the buyers and vice versa. Each one regarded the other as stupid.

After so many years of isolation since the Revolution, the Russians discovered a new world and the world discovered the Russians. It was as if a curtain had been raised. We Jews who had experienced life under the Nazis did not dare to criticize; rather, we were happy and thankful to be able to live in freedom. That much we appreciated. We tended to see everything as positive and were careful not to make any negative remarks, nor to tell jokes. Even humor could be dangerous.

But my friends and I saw ourselves as being in a hopeless situation. We therefore decided to go to Russia voluntarily. For outsiders like us it was not easy to reach the "center of paradise". We reported for registration and had to wait all night before being examined and finally accepted. We were assigned to the coal-mining district of Donbas. Happy and content, we went home. A few days later we were to present ourselves at the railway station in Brest from where we would be sent to our destination. I told my friends of my good luck and, with a knapsack on my back, reported to the station at the scheduled time. There were hundreds who had gathered to be transported. Among them were my friends Simon Levender and Alter Engelman. But then like a bolt of lightning, Mrs. Weißgroß appeared at my side. She had lived in our neighborhood for years, knew my family and claimed that she had even been at my Brit-Milah.

She took me aside and said that she could not let me go to Russia, from where her sons and relatives had just returned. She claimed to know the truth and therefore her conscience could not accept my going there alone. She had also tried to persuade my friends, but had had no success with them. Perhaps she had not attended their Brit-Milahs. My two friends did not change their minds and on that evening left by convoy for Russia, while I returned to the city with Mrs. Weißgroß. I never saw my friends or Mrs. Weißgroß again. I later learned from their relatives that they had died in Russia.

Now I was entirely alone, without a roof over my head and any means of supporting myself. I was homesick and longed to be with my family, regardless of whether my homeland was occupied by the communists or the Nazis. Since I saw no future for me in Brest I decided to go home. I traveled by train to the border where I met other people with the same intention. The Russians gathered us into groups. We told them that we had just come from the German side. That was reason enough to be sent back. I do not know whether they believed our story, but in any case they showed understanding and patience.

As soon as we reached the other side of the border, we scattered, each one of us going his own way. I returned home and was welcomed like a long-lost son. I have often asked myself whether my returning home was right. I was to regret it many times later.

It did not take long for the Russians to start sending all so-called "western refugees", i.e. those from the occupied part of Poland, to the east. Usually they ended up in Siberia, in work camps or prisons, and were treated as deportees and convicts according to Russian law. We exchanged letters with the ones we knew for a while. Life was difficult there, but they were neither tortured nor exterminated.

In their letters one often sensed a longing for house and home; some even envied us because we had stayed home. No wonder. Who could imagine, without having lived through it, what it meant to be a Jew in the so-called General Government under the Nazi murderers?

When the Russo-German war started, all connections with the so-called "deportees" were broken off. It did not take much longer until even they knew that we were only to be pitied.

5 - Life in Radzyn

Life in Radzyn slowly returned to normal, if one can speak of normal conditions at all during such a time. After the Jews had been driven out of their beautiful houses on the market square and from the better areas of the city, a new Jewish quarter was established in the worst part of the city, where the poorest Jews already lived. This area was crossed by many narrow streets such as Kozia, Sholna, and Kalen.

The Judenrat under the strict leadership of David Lichtenstein functioned well, given the circumstances. It was composed primarily of highly-respected members of the Jewish community. The majority of the Jewish police was also comprised of respectable, young people. Compared with what one heard about other towns, the Jews of Radzyn hardly had any reason to feel ashamed of their community leaders.

But like almost everywhere else, we also had no particular reason to be proud. People were irritated. Each day was more difficult than the day before with Fridays being the worst. Every Friday, the Sicherheitsdienst presented a package of decrees and laws to the Judenrat, which were to be imposed on the community immediately. The laws were to be put into effect within a week, since a new package always arrived on the following Friday. These detested decrees and laws were devised for one purpose only: to torment and decimate us Jews. With every new week, life became more burdensome and more unbearable. The work which was partly ordered by the Judenrat also became more intolerable because of the chicanery and excesses of some of the SS sadists involved. The number of attacks on individual apartments at night increased. They included robbery, destruction and murder.

One night some SD people broke into the apartment of Mr. Scheinmann. Eli Scheinmann was a respectable Zionist askan. His wife was intelligent and well educated. His son was my friend and schoolmate; we grew up together. As they were being beaten by the SD people, Mrs. Scheinmann resisted and allegedly slapped one of the SD men. She and her husband were shot on the spot. Their son, my friend, was able to flee, but was later shot too. I will never forget the long discussions we had as schoolchildren with that intelligent woman. May her memory be honored!

7 p.m. was the curfew time Jews, when all gates and doors had to be shut. For the Poles the curfew was later, at 9 p.m. Windows facing the street were blacked out so as not to attract the attention of the Germans. Night assaults were, however, quite normal. Often Jews were removed from their apartments and placed in inadequate accommodations in the poor section of town. In the still of the night, the spiked boots of German patrols consisting of two or four soldiers could be heard clearly. As soon as they approached, all lights were turned off and there was a deathly silence. We breathed again only when their footsteps could no longer be heard.

We were ordered to wear white bands with a Judenstern on our right sleeves. Failure to comply meant death. Leaving an apartment and entering another house was prohibited. Despite this order, neighbors came together in their backyards to visit each other. Hardly anyone dared to walk on the street, since the soldiers fired immediately. But what transpired in the back of the houses could not be seen from the outside. There we could read newspapers and talk about them openly. Radios had been confiscated a long time ago. Owning or listening to a radio was punishable by death.

Backyard meetings took place almost every night, with the discussion continuing the next day at work or whenever or wherever an opportunity presented itself. In this way we encouraged and strengthened each other. There were several intelligent people in the town who dedicated themselves to this task and, in so doing, provided help to many. They had neither bound themselves to this chore nor were they organized. To help morally was simply the wish of all the people who suffered in this desperate situation. I still remember one quiet hero, Levy Levi. He was a shoemaker by trade, but also a self-taught man and intelligent and religious. A Ben Torah who often led the congregation on the Holy Days. His commentaries were well known and were a balm to our hearts. We also knew that he was right in predicting Hitler's end, but in regard to the point of time, he was mistaken.

Our house, too, was a meeting place. At night we sat together in semi-darkness. Mrs. Kalinka came with her son and beautiful daughter, with whom I had a brief love affair that soon ended with her resettlement. Resettlement was the name of the deadly game. There was Benjamin Kupiec, a wood merchant, who lived in the neighborhood, and the Kaweblum family. We talked and told jokes which often brought tears of laughter. Every now and then a relative or acquaintance came from another town to spend the night. We told each other what was happening, comparing the suffering. Benjamin Kupiec was fortunate to die a natural death from illness. I also remember Benjamin's sister-in-law, the wife of Mendel Kupiec. During a deportation Aktion her child was accidentally smothered when they were hiding in a cellar, out of fear that the child's cries and sobs would lead to detection. When she was eventually discovered and came out of hiding, the only thing she held in her hands was a flower pot.

All Jews were subject to forced labor without payment. In the early mornings the groups of workers gathered in front of the Judenrat on Koziastraße. Those who had a permanent position were practically treated as privileged Jews; they went mostly alone or marched to work in groups. The rest, the majority of those gathered, were lined up in rows by the Jewish police who then led them to their positions. They were always accompanied by the Jewish police, the Polish police or the Germans.

The Judenrat made every possible effort to meet the demands of the Germans in order to avoid spontaneous Aktionen. Their success was only limited. It was impossible to prevent the authorities from exploiting and humiliating their Jewish victims as they saw fit. Depending on their mood and desire, they took Jews out of their homes, their backyards, their beds and the streets, wherever they saw them. They enjoyed showing the superiority of their race over the Jewish Untermenschen.

The work crews consisted of men, women and adolescents. Sometimes they were mixed, sometimes separated according to sex. Some were forcibly recruited by the Judenrat; some Jews were so poor that they allowed themselves to be given any work by the Judenrat in order to earn their daily bread. Moreover, this was the only opportunity to get out of the Jewish quarter, come in contact with Christians, and perhaps find something to eat, since nothing was produced in the Jewish district. Those poor people who depended on payments from the Judenrat were especially vulnerable to arbitrary treatment. Anyone who had money was able to redeem himself. Thus, a privileged class developed and nepotism flourished. The families of Judenrat members and the Jewish Police were exempt from forced labor. Consequently, hatred and hostility toward them grew.

The people in the work crews looked poor and shabby. Their clothes were worn and patched; pants were made mostly of dyed canvas, fur trimmings had been removed from the winter coats, which were drawn together with a string around the waist for warmth or to smuggle a turnip or some bread back into the Jewish section. Women and girls who were not accustomed to such hard work developed rough faces, cracked lips and swollen legs from the wind and bad weather. It was a pitiful sight, especially seeing acquaintances that one was used to seeing in quite a different light. Only on Sundays, if it was quiet and no work was required, did people look at themselves in a mirror and try to restore the looks of their former selves.

Those who had redeemed themselves from the Judenrat were only safe from the Jewish police. Their redemption was hardly accepted by the Germans, so they were forced to hide. No one could move about freely in the streets of the Jewish district during the day, and at night it was prohibited in any case. Although Radzyn was not a fenced-in ghetto with barbed wire, hardly anyone dared to leave the Jewish section. Venturing outside always meant trouble and maybe even danger to one's life. It was especially risky for a Jew to walk past the houses of the Gestapo and other police offices, but also the Rathaus, the castle, the house of Wieckowski or the former house of Catholic priests which was across from the house of M. Apeloig, facing Gestapo headquarters. For no reason at all a Jew could be taken in and never come back. At best one was made a target of ridicule and beaten.

The general food supply was divided into three categories. Only members of the "master race" and their collaborators were amply sustained. The Poles got almost enough. We Jews were never regularly provided with food. Our rations were distributed sporadically, in small quantities, and only in exchange for ration coupons. The food we received was always of poor quality or spoiled. We were condemned to starvation by both the legislators and the occupation forces. Those who did not want to starve were forced to rely on bartering and smuggling.

Jews were excluded from any social or medical care. Hospitals did not accept Jews. Medicine could only be obtained through subterfuge. Jewish stores were closed or confiscated and taken over by ethnic German or Polish trustees. Most Jews were removed from their former jobs. They were not allowed to accept a contract of employment. The jobs reserved for us were cutting wood, carrying water and similar menial activities. We lived outside society and outside the law. Nevertheless, we found time to comfort each other and to laugh. The Poles had not exactly spoiled us either. We believed and hoped that we would survive the Germans despite their persecution.

Between the frequent Aktionen against Jews, which always ended in the same way, there were quiet periods which sometimes lasted only a few days, but at times two to three weeks. The survivors crawled out of their hideouts and used the time for stocking up on food. On those quiet days one saw Polish farmers coming into the Jewish district early in the morning or at night when the Germans were not there; they sneaked into Jewish houses with small packages of food and came out with big packages.

Many Jews gave Polish friends their best pieces of clothing, furniture, or household goods or anything they had been able to save in exchange for something to eat or to have the Poles take care of their belongings until the war was over. These oral agreements were usually made without any guarantees and under the guise of humanity and neighborly love. On one side, there was Jewish misery and helplessness and, on the other, Polish greed and cunning. The business of safekeeping until after the war flourished. Heated competition developed between Polish peasants, each one trying to accumulate more Jewish possessions than the other.

Many of these Poles were very poor and lived in misery. Some were still living in chattas with straw roofs, no flooring and sparse or primitive furniture. They often ate with wooden spoons and slept on straw mattresses with pillows and bedding made of chequered ticking without covers. Their clothes were tattered, often ripped or patched. The only suit and pair of shoes they owned were worn to church on Sunday.

Suddenly, moderately wealthy Jewish homes with good furniture, damask bed linen, real silverware and modern clothing were opened to them, offering riches about which they had never dreamed. For a mere sandwich or a kind word, they could have these desirable items from the hungry and worried Jews. Typical portable Jewish valuables of that time were: two silver Sabbath candlesticks, plush quilts used for covering the beds and a gold necklace, which was usually already gone by then. From the very beginning we Jews were deprived of all gold by the Gestapo, either directly through forced contributions or by means of the Judenrat under the threat of deportation or shooting. These objects belonged to the household and were the status symbols of a Jewish middle-class family. Only in the event of extreme desperation could these items be touched. And desperation was everywhere now. If one were not forced to trade them for a piece of bread, then they were given to the farmers for safekeeping until after the war. One can safely assume that all such candlesticks and quilts found anywhere in rural Poland today were once Jewish possessions.

The numerous poor Jews did not have these problems. Even they possessed Sabbath candlesticks, but they were small and made of brass and their quilts were not plush.

I will never forget a typical scene when Poles wanted to buy or just take the clothes we Jews were wearing. They used the following argument: "Give me the suit you have on. It will be taken from you soon anyway before they kill you." Who can imagine how our hearts felt when we heard that?

Almost everyone, including my family, entrusted household items and clothing to farmers for safekeeping. When we noticed our mistake, it was too late. When I was the last one of my family who remained, I did not give away a single other thing for safekeeping. I sold everything I could and just left the rest. I have never regretted this decision; sometimes I have actually been proud of it.

Very few of these rural Polish "saviors" were actually helpful, most of them were merely opportunists. Innumerable Jews were later beaten and murdered by their "saviors" for their valuables.

Today we know these illegally obtained objects hardly brought joy to the Polish people.

Jewish children played a special, almost heroic part in the struggle for daily bread and existence. A child could get through more easily and was not recognized as quickly. For that reason, they were often depended upon for finding food. At an early age they became the breadwinners of the family and they performed that task beautifully.

There were no schools for Jewish children. Books and schools were taboo. It is no exaggeration to say that in a certain sense there were no children among us. They grew up prematurely and became, in a way, what their parents meant them to be. In the evening after work, if everyone returned home in good health, those who stayed home all day were always thankful and joyous. In numerous families, children went to work to provide for their old and sick parents. These distressed people watched at the window, counting the minutes, waiting hour after hour until they finally had their beloved children back. It was heartbreaking when they returned beaten, wounded or sometimes not at all. They were satisfied when the youngsters smuggled in some food. They went to bed hungry if the food was taken from the children at the Gate Kontrolle.

Every day was a war itself – a battle for one's relatives, life, food and health. It had never been easy for us, and now it had grown even more difficult. But by comparison with what followed, it was tolerable.

We young people gradually organized ourselves and formed a new Hevra of about ten to twelve young boys and girls from a former group, most of whom had stayed in Radzyn. As often as possible –

especially on Sundays – we met secretly, usually at the Kamienietzki sisters' apartment. Because they were so-called "useful" Jews, they had a larger apartment than any of the rest of us. The two sisters sewed clothes, underwear and other things for the SD officials and their wives. In their apartment, we sang our old songs softly, talked and helped each other bear the hardships of life. We discussed developments and agreed not to become people who benefited at the cost of others. We thought ahead and even made plans for our future survival.

Since Radzyn was the county seat and boasted a big castle and several luxurious houses, it became the headquarters of the Gestapo, SD, Gendarmerie, Schutzpolizei and the county commissioner's office. All of these authorities made enormous demands on the small Jewish community through the Judenrat. The Jews were tasked with cutting wood, carrying water, cleaning toilets, shining boots, providing coal and firewood, maintaining houses, cleaning cars, sweeping roads, grooming horses, burying the dead bodies of people who were tortured and killed etc. Beyond that, we repeatedly had to allocate large amounts of money as so-called "contributions". We also had to provide coffee, tea, gold, watches, jewelry, underwear, leather, fur coats, boots, suits, butter, eggs and geese. The last three items had to be contributed several times, for birthdays, holidays etc.

Coming up with the required goods became increasingly difficult. Jews were not allowed to leave their houses or establish contact with the world outside, not even with the Polish population. The rations allocated to us became every small; for dying they were too much, yet for living not enough – later they were stopped altogether.

Our tormentors made a sport of chasing us out of one apartment and into another. This constant moving to a worse apartment can greatly burden a human being physically and psychologically, since each move entailed losing at least part of one's possessions or irreplaceable valuables that had been hidden. That each change of residence had to be made within a few hours was a matter of course for the Nazis; for us, however, it meant special hardship. I still remember our big wardrobe, which we never took apart or moved till the Germans marched in. It took us an entire day to disassemble and rebuild it. Later, having moved so often, we were able to do it in an hour. The massive lower part with the heavy drawers could be opened only while sitting; the upper part was bulky and solid, as were the side walls and the heavy carved doors. Today such an antique would have great value.

In addition to the Nazis, anti-Semites of Polish and Ukrainian origin circled us like vultures, waiting for their prey to die. In Radzyn, a Ukrainian mayor was appointed, whose name I do not remember, but whose face I shall never forget. He was emaciated, had thin lips, deeply-set, small eyes and never laughed – above all he was a fanatical anti-Semite. His character was reflected in his face. Apparently this armchair sadist found his only satisfaction in hating and torturing the Jews. For him, the anti-Jewish Aktionen of the Nazis were neither fast nor strict enough. He had a Polish assistant named Domakowski. Domakowski was a refugee, who confiscated an apartment in the Jewish house of the Schuchmacher family, which was a few houses away from us. He was strong and tough and a practicing anti-Semite.

Commissioned by the town, he confiscated Jewish property, including apartments and houses, without the slightest consideration. He literally took everything he desired for himself. Regardless of the time of day or night, whenever he needed or wanted something, he would go to a Jewish home and take it. During the pillages he often became violent and struck people. It was not so much the confiscated items that interested him, but rather the pleasure he derived from taking them. The mayor and his assistant Domakowski lived on our suffering. The head of the Judenrat tried to tame these two beasts too, but only with modest success. They intended to keep abreast of the Gestapo.

As if we did not have enough problems, we also had to endure sporadic raids from the SS and police units from other areas. During one of these raids my brother was caught and taken away. For a week we heard not a word from him, nor did we know where he was being held. Finally we learned that he was in the camp at Belzec, about 120 kilometers south of Radzyn. Like Sobibor, Belzec was one of the testing areas for the later concentration camps. We tried every possible way to free him, but in vain. After a few weeks he came back. He had managed to escape under unbelievable circumstances, walking through fields and woods at night and hiding during the day so as not to be discovered. He described the unbelievable torture which Jews suffered at the camp at the hands of SS sadists. A "Dolf" or "Wolf" about whom he told us must have been an animal in human form. My brother returned psychologically beaten, dirty, full of lice, half-starved and dull-witted. But he had returned, and we were overwhelmed with joy. He needed weeks to become a normal person again, but our persecutors did not give us much time.

During that period my friend Zwi Apeloig came to visit. Shortly after the war had broken out, Zwi fled to the part of Poland that was occupied by the Russians. Because he was not able to integrate there, he had migrated to the center of Russia. After he became acquainted with the situation in the Russian paradise, he decided, out of desperation, to return home to Radzyn. After crossing the River Bug, he arrived in Wlodowa where the Schutzpolizei and Gendarmerie from Radzyn were carrying out an Aktion. The police units which were stationed in Radzyn executed daily Aktionen again Jews within a radius of about 100 kilometers.

We could tell from Zwi's face what he had experienced: it was distorted and he looked grief-stricken, and his eyes were full of tears. Everything seemed to emerge from within. He could not free himself from the scenes he had witnessed: a mass execution of Jews – men, women and children; the streets full of blood from the dead and injured. What he described was unbelievable. Although he had come back to his family out of desperation and had planned to stay with them, he eventually decided to return to Russia. By then it had become difficult to cross the border, but he was lucky.

He survived the stint in Russia and is living in Israel today. He later told me in Israel how lucky he was to meet an Austrian from Vienna, a previous Social Democrat, now a border guard, trying to help Jews. The guard actually brought my friend across the border, helping a Jew and acting against Hitler.

I was fortunate because I was considered a "useful" Jew. The elder of the Jews had a son, Simon Lichtenstein, who had studied electronics in Paris and had returned shortly before the war broke out. With my manual skills and his connections, we organized ourselves with a common desire to survive and became responsible for the electrical work in all the German offices, along with other small jobs. Compared with what others did, my job was not too difficult; it enabled me to earn some money and to organize a few things. The work we did for the Wehrmacht was sometimes paid for by the local paymaster. The Gestapo and the police units did not contribute anything. They paid for our work by not killing us, at least not yet. Sometimes, but seldom, we received a piece of bread or meat for performing some special task or in trade.

My father lived by means of his contacts with Polish acquaintances, usually landed proprietors with whom he had previously done business. Some did not forget us and helped purely for humanitarian reasons; others, however, put us out of their minds. But like other Jews, my father was forced to do anything he could to survive.

During that period we were once again evicted from our apartment, which was given to the Niewyrozumski family. Our whole family was forced to move into a one-room apartment in the same house. Mr. Niewyrozumski, a Pole, was the former director of the local elementary school. Apparently he had good connections with the

SD; soon after Himmler ordered the schools to close, he was made director of the town's dairy and of the distribution office for tobacco and cigarettes. Those were very high positions during the war, when everything was scarce and rationed, and the black market flourished.

A business relationship was established between Niewyrozumski and my father. From time to time the Pole passed him cigarettes through an attic door for which he received money. My father then sold the cigarettes to a middleman who in turn sold them to someone else. One day when several such middlemen were arrested, they revealed their sources. Nothing happened to Mr. Niewyrozumski; my father, however, was arrested.

On the day of his apprehension an entire world came to an end for me and my family. I withdrew from everything. When I did not have to work, I hid at home or outside. We did everything possible to secure my father's release. But all our efforts through the Judenrat with payments of money and valuables and all our attempts through connections with the authorities were in vain. We couldn't get him released. After two or three weeks, my father was transferred to the prison at Lublin. He was to be tried by a so-called Sondergericht (special court). One of only two acceptable lawyers in the Sondergericht was the well-known Hofmokl Ostrowski, who had offices in Warsaw and Cracow. We turned to him and he agreed to defend my father for a large sum of money. I was chosen to correspond with him because it was impossible to meet with him personally. Jews were forbidden to travel.

6 - Father and Brother in Lublin Prison

On a Friday morning in December of 1941, my brother and I went out to clean the snow from the front of the house. Suddenly we saw the dog of the Gestapo chief, Fischer, in the distance. We knew that a four-legged harasser, trained to attack Jews, was inevitably followed by a two-legged one.

My brother said quietly, "Let's go! This time they are looking for me!" The night before another big raid had taken place; many Poles, among them our neighbor, the former officer Borkowski, and some Jews had been arrested. We knew that, while arresting one person, the Gestapo liked to take along close relatives as well, regardless of whether they were guilty or innocent. Every arrest by the Gestapo meant certain torture and death. I did not know how my brother was connected with the raid or with the arrested Borkowski nor which charges were being brought against him. They could be things such as reading and distributing underground papers. I knew, however, that my brother and Borkowski were friends and had often spoken to each other. My brother must have been a thorn in the Gestapo's eye for another reason. He was tall, broad-shouldered, strong and in good health. He was the opposite of the typical Jew as described in the Stürmer, the slanderous anti-Semitic newspaper. My brother's physical appearance contradicted the Nazi's racial theory. That was enough reason to eliminate any such Jew.

After catching sight of the Gestapo dog we ran away and hid in a barn. We were later told that the SD official Adolf Deckhoff, an ethnic German of gruesome character and a well-known Jew killer, proceeded with two other SD officials and the dog directly to our apartment. This took place a few weeks after my father's arrest. Both my mother and sister Idessa were sick and in bed. The SD men asked for my brother, then demolished everything within their reach and left an order that my brother Meier must report to the Gestapo no later than Monday morning at seven o'clock. Adolf Dickhoff and his colleagues then went to the house of the Judenrat, called together all the members present at that time and repeated his command that my brother appear before the Gestapo the next Monday morning. If the order was not obeyed, the entire Judenrat (twelve members) and one hundred Jews from the town would be shot.

This order was a grave misfortune for the town's Jewish population and especially for our family. The alternatives we faced were horrible. Either we had to deliver my brother to his murderers or have the deaths of 112 men on our consciences, not to mention the suffering of the widows and orphans. Several members of the Judenrat and the Jewish police soon came to our house. Some of them implored, some threatened, others pitied us. Friends, relatives, Torah scholars – all of them wanted to help, but none knew how. Nobody doubted the seriousness of the threat.

That evening, after dark, we left our hiding place in the barn. My brother found a safer spot in the attic of Eli-Chaim Tenenbaum's house. I hid close to our apartment in Alter Kaschemacher's house, from where I could watch the entrance to our apartment through an attic window. My brother had the added burden of hiding from the Jewish police. I, however, sneaked into our place at night to be with my mother and sister. We sat in the dim light with the shutters closed, believing that together we could bear our suffering more easily. On that unforgettably Friday, my mother lit the Sabbath candles as usual and, following Jewish custom, covered her eyes to say the prayer. The silence was broken by weeping and sighs. My two sisters, my brother-in-law, their child and I stood helplessly around the table with heads hanging down and tears in our eyes. We were five tortured, helpless and worried people who could only be saved by God. A long time passed after the prayer before my mother uncovered her eyes. Her face was no longer the same. Her eyes were swollen and red; they expressed what was going on inside her. There was so much she had to pray for.

Today I still choke on my tears when I think of it. I wanted to be allowed to cry then, but I had to remain strong. We felt as if we had all been sentenced to death and had to await our execution. The room was filled with a deadly silence, each one of us immersed in our own thoughts. Only the ticking of the clock and the pounding of our hearts were audible. A quick death would have been a relief.

It was cruel enough when the Gestapo picked up its victims, but at least one did not have to blame oneself. It was our misfortune to be chosen and thereby punished further by delivering our victims ourselves. The beast did not only want our blood, he wanted to be served by us as well. We received my brother's death sentence (by registered mail) from the Gestapo with an ultimatum. The ultimatum had a time limit of 72 hours – we had only that much time to think. To live with this knowledge – that was the tragedy for my mother and my family. I cannot describe my brother's feelings. I only know that he did not want to decide alone and waited for the counsel and help of the family.

Early Monday morning, my mother, my two sisters and I want to Meier's hiding place. My mother suffered the most, not only because of her maternal feelings, but because her son insisted upon a decision from her and was willing to obey her unconditionally.

During our visit no one offered advice or discussed anything. Instead, we just enjoyed looking at each other and feeling together. That was our hunger which had to be appeased at that moment. It was an indescribable consolation in such a horrendous situation. Our eyes filled with tears of sorrow and joy – sorrow about our separation and the joy of being together, if only momentarily. We ignored the future, even if it was only for a few moments. We looked at each other continually as we hugged and kissed.

My mother managed to utter the words expected of her: "My child, I do not know what you should do, but whatever you decide, may god be with you." I am sure that these words were not planned. They were simply an extemporaneous expression of her thoughts at the moment.

We embraced and kissed: no one was able to speak. It was the last time that we were able to do so. Only my father was not there; he was in jail, but soon other members of our family would be missing.

My brother arose, left his hideout and went to the barber. He had his head shaved in order to avoid the first part of the Gestapo routine. From there he went to the Gestapo. He was 27 years old. We never saw him again. After a short time he was transferred to the castle prison at Lublin along with Chaim Diamant, Isser Sonnenschein and many others. My father and brother were in the same prison, but my father did not know it. There was a chance that we might see our father again, but we knew there was no hope for my brother. I know today that he was tortured mercilessly.

We continued our attempts to liberate my father. Eventually we managed to contact him. Some prison guards smuggled messages for us. To conceal my brother's arrest from my father, I signed the messages with my brother's name. After work I spent all night writing letters to Mr. Hofmokl Ostrowski, the prominent lawyer of German origin. I hardly slept. I spent each night thinking and dreaming. Ostrowski's letters were short and few. He was our only hope and at least he showed understanding for our situation which in turn encouraged me to write more letters.

The day of my father's trail finally arrived. He was accused of smuggling cigarettes. The fact that he was a Jew was not emphasized, which was fortunate for us. The trial was held in Lublin, but we could travel there only with special permission. I will never forget the night before the trial. I was reared in a traditional Jewish-Zionist household, but we were not particularly religious. That night I did nothing except read the Psalms. I had to do something and I could think of nothing better or more appropriate. My knowledge of Hebrew was sufficient to understand most of the text. I did not only read, I prayed, sobbed, implored and swore every single word. This was my way of praying to God; I did not want to lose my father.

As a kind of compensation for the head of my brother, the elder of the Jews provided my mother and sister with special permission to travel to Lublin for the trial. It was mid-February – cold and icy. My mother and sister traveled in a state of complete desperation. As though that wasn't enough, in Lublin my mother slipped on the icy street and broke her hand. Despite the intense pain she still managed to attend the trial. My father was sentenced to four months in prison, but because of Mr. Ostrowski's connections, he was released from serving the remainder of the sentence (two to three weeks). The lawyer asked my mother who had written the impressive letters.

My father returned with mother. Our happiness was overwhelming. Even greater was the sensational news that a Jew had returned alive and well from a German prison. Relatives and acquaintances came with congratulations; it was a happy event in a time of predominant sorrow. I thought about the numerous letters I had written which were actually meant as a prayer to God, but were directed to the lawyer who understood them correctly. It had been exceedingly difficult, but it had not been in vain.

It was 1942, shortly after the decisions of the Wannsee Conference had started to make themselves felt. The former Nazi method of torturing Jews to death was replaced by capital punishment in accordance with the Endlösung. The first mass execution following the new rules was supposed to take place in the castle prison at Lublin. As far as I remember, witnesses reported that on February 17, 1942 all or the majority of the Jews imprisoned there were brought together and shot. According to the same testimony my brother was shot on that day. Only one day before, on February 16,

1942, my father was released without knowing that his son was in the same prison. We at home could only cry over the rescue of my father and the loss of my brother.

7 - New Laws and New Forms of Abuse

My father came home a changed man. He was older and hardly spoke at all. The Nazis did not give us time for that. Neither did we have time to rejoice over our father's rescue, or mourn my lost brother; we were emotionally, physically and morally overcome by this new series of bitter events.

In the town and the surrounding areas, mass arrests of Jews and Poles became more frequent. New groups of prisoners arrived daily. The prison was overflowing. Almost every day people that had been tortured to death were turned over to the Judenrat not only for burial, but also as a deterrent. The building of the former municipal authorities, in the back of which a prison had been set up, now became the Gestapo's slaughterhouse in which hundreds of people were harassed, tortured and then buried in the backyard. Jews were usually given "the honor" of digging the graves.

Through my work for the German authorities, I once visited this building by coincidence. I saw the wall spattered with blood, whips, instruments of torture and the special tables for beatings; I also heard the cries of tortured people. They still ring in my ears today. One of the sadistic SD officials was Auenstein, a choleric, brutal character, whose name and voice I will never forget. The names Heyn, Kaiser and Engels have also stayed with me.

Friday was the worst day of the week because of the laws and decrees issued against us. Everything seemed to confirm the existence of an organization that invented new anti-Jewish laws every week. One of these Fridays brought the so-called fur decree. We Jews were not allowed to own furs, since they were sorely needed by the triumphant German army, which in the meantime was freezing to death in Russia. The order required, among other things, that we turn over not only fur clothing, but also every piece of fur and all other materials which resembled fur, be it from a sleeve or hats or a decorative element on a dress. Violations were punishable by death. At that time Jews owned hardly any fur, since most of it had already been exchanged for food. Nevertheless, this order gave the Nazis a new excuse to shoot Jews.

One day some Gestapo agents came to our neighbor, the hairdresser Mr. Neumann. They claimed that they had smelled burned fur and therefore proceeded to shoot Mrs. Neumann and her daughter. This kind of fur Aktion was responsible for many deaths in the town.

Repeatedly we were told of new arrests and shootings. For example, Berl Lichtenstein, who was called Mydlarnik, was turned over to the Judenrat for burial after having been sewn inside a straw mattress. During the internment someone discovered that he was still alive. But on orders from the Gestapo he had to be buried immediately anyway.

The former driver Berl Joel, who had worked his way up to stable master under the Gestapo, was the person most often commissioned to transfer the dead bodies to the Judenrat for burial. The relatives of those who were arrested and murdered often recognized clothes as those of their loved ones. Joel was suspected of cooperating with the Gestapo. Everyone was afraid of him. It did not take long, however, before even this "hero" was shot by the Gestapo. We sighed with relief and almost felt satisfaction at his death. We regarded this incident as a good act.

For the Nazis, this was the time of their lives. Having absolute authority, they could take and make use of anything that belonged to Jews. Thus, it happened that a captain of the Schutzpolizei became attracted to a very pretty, young Jewish girl, who apparently stole his heart. Because of the captain's affection, the girl was able to live better and more securely than other Jews.

She was seductively beautiful and soon got to know other police officers. On a rank with the elder of the Jews, she advanced to the position of Stadlanut. She tried to help as much as possible with regard to work, Aktionen against Jews and other of our troubles. Our Miss F. was something of a small Queen Esther. I doubted, however, that this little queen knew anything about the Nuremberg racial laws. As a man, one could understand how the proud captain regarded Rassenschande (racial disgrace) as a burden, but forgot it when he was close to her.

One day, one of her friends and protectors showed up at her apartment. I do not know how long he stayed but when he left, she lay dead in her bed in a pool of blood. He had shot her in that part of her body where he had probably enjoyed her the most. Thus, he was saved from being tried for Rassenschande.

Thanks to our work for the German authorities, Simon and I had the unique opportunity to see a movie made for German soldiers in the Scala Theater. The theater had belonged to a Jewish woman, but of course it had been confiscated and was now reserved exclusively for members of the German Wehrmacht. The place was full of soldiers. The film was Jud Süß. What impressed me most, however, was the newsreel.

It must have been 1941, shortly after the German invasion of Latvia and Lithuania. The audience, mostly from the Wehrmacht, was shown how their triumphant German brothers conquered Riga, entered the local synagogue, gathered the Jews, desecrated the building and unrolled the Torahs on the floor and trampled them. The Baltic Jews were then forced to do the same and were ridiculed and abused. Finally, the synagogue was set on fire. The laughing soldiers on the screen, the bellowed comments from the audience and the poisonous tin voice of the newsreader still echo in my ears today.

Around that time, the SD official Engels, a man from the Rhineland, called down to me from his window: "Hey, Jew, come here." I entered his house. He had just arisen and was not yet entirely dressed. He ordered me to sit on a stool and gave me shoe polish, a brush and a cloth. He lay, actually lay, down in a deep, soft chair, stretched out his legs with his booted feet in front of my face and commanded: "Jew, shine my boots!" I set to work. He then started talking: "What actually are you, you Jew? You are not a dog, or a horse, or an animal, but then, you are not a human being either. You are just a Jew...a Jew..." I kept silent and tried to control myself, not showing my feelings. In the meantime he noticed that his boots were ready. He got up and dismissed me with the dignity of his belief in the master race. He neither thanked me nor gave me the expected kick. He simply said, "Go away, Jew!" I left and did not even feel humiliated, but this incident gave me cause for reflection. What kind of a monster was that, and what kind of diabolical ideas did he have that enabled him to order a human being to shine his boots and to carry on such a conversation? What kind of perversion, sadism or ideology moved such a person?

A large part of the town's Jewish population was working to build a military airfield at Marianki, about 5-10 kilometers from Radzyn. This airport was built in a hurry to aid the invasion of Russia. People worked day and night. Due to bad nutrition and insufficient clothing, they suffered greatly from the cold. Jews were only used for hard labor and had to fight with pick and shovel against the frozen ground. Depending on the mood of a particular guard, they were either tortured or "just" badly treated. Despite everything, this was a tolerable transition period, since one had a feeling of doing something useful. It also gave us a right to live. This usefulness was turned to financial advantage by the Judenrat. After the invasion of Russia, the Germans abandoned the airfield; work was stopped and we were deprived of the hope of working and maintaining the accompanying security.

Despite our disastrous situation, we never forgot how to laugh. For months a decree was enforced that required all Jews to salute German soldiers by taking off their hats. Naturally it often happened that a soldier on the other side of the street was overlooked and not saluted. Some Jews were beaten for that. To avoid breaking this law, we decided to take off and put on our caps continually while walking down the streets. Our strategy was soon discovered and regarded as ridicule and disrespect for the German uniform. Consequently, saluting a German soldier was outlawed and enforced by capital punishment. Only laughing was not yet punishable by death. Not yet being the pertinent phrase.

One day while the saluting decree was still in effect, I rode past an on-duty Gendarme without saluting him or taking off my cap. Because of my job, I was privileged enough to be allowed to ride a bicycle during working hours. Reaching for his carbine, he called me back, slapped my face and ordered me to pass him ten times, each time taking off my cap. I did what he demanded, but without looking at him. In the end I did it twelve times.

The offices of the Judenrat were on Koziakalenstrasse. Moreh Horaha had previously lived there and it came with a small house of prayer. Lichtenstein, the elder of the Jews, lived in our neighborhood in the house of the Slimak family. Jewish men and women often came to him with their problems, which occasionally produced some shocking scenes. Through my connection with Lichtenstein's son Simon, I frequently visited their apartment, where I saw and heard a few things. Once I saw a package being prepared for mailing. It contained gold, jewelry and other valuables and was addressed to "Fischer in Erfurt". Fischer was the Gestapo chief of Radzyn town and district. I noted the city Erfurt; Fischers' name I did not have to write down, since I could never forget it. But I will come back to this story later.

Now only the present counted. Getting through daily life was our main occupation. It was only important to protect oneself from beatings, pain and abuse, to have enough food and to stay alive. Every Jew, regardless of age and sex, was waging this battle.

After our preoccupation with my father and the mourning of my brother, a new tragedy befell our family. My aunt, Chaya Turkeltaub, had hidden out of fear of a forthcoming Aktion against Jews. Her hideout was a Polish farm in the village of Zabikow, about 6 kilometers from Radzyn. I do not know whether it happened by accident or during a search, but she was found, recognized as a Jew, and shot immediately. The Gendarmerie continued its search in other houses, where they discovered another two older Jewish women, Mrs. Geliebter and Mrs. Steinberg, whom they also shot. When we received news of the tragic events, my cousin Mendl Turkeltaub and relatives of the other murdered women hired a Polish driver with a horse-drawn wagon and proceeded to the village to retrieve the corpses and bury them at the Jewish cemetery in Radzyn. The same Gendarme stopped the wagon when it approached the village, asked the three passengers what they wanted and then, having identified them as Jews, shot them. Later the Judenrat was also denied permission to bury our murdered. Their bodies remained on the roadside, superficially covered with dirt by some farmers.

These murders, especially the way in which the seven innocent people – three older women, three or four young men – were killed, upset the Jewish population of the town. The farmers of the village and the Polish driver told us that the murderers belonged to a Gendarmerie unit where most of the members came from Hamburg. We saw these men every day. They looked like everyone else, but they were killers, killers in uniform.

We felt deep grief and we wept for our dead. Everyone felt like a victim, since we knew that each bullet was directed at every person of Jewish faith and ancestry. My aunt had been a modest, meticulous woman who was deeply loved by her husband and son. Her only son had been killed on the same day by the same murderers.

Her husband, Uncle Nathan, who normally had a good sense of humor, changed completely. He suffered and reacted differently to most others. As a religious Jew, he had kept a kosher house, prayed every day and gone regularly to the synagogue. From that day on, however, he purposely did everything that is forbidden according to the Jewish religion. He was not only disappointed in people but in God as well. He had the courage to say what many only thought. Nobody contradicted him – everybody showed understanding. His famous sense of humor disappeared. He no longer told stories about the ten years he spent in Russia as a soldier of the Czar or joked about the shtetl and its characters. He did not understand the world anymore. His vitality was dissipated; he no longer fought for his life. He used his energy only for insolence. Despite the prohibitions, he ventured outside the town without the required armband and from one such misadventure he never returned. In this way his wish not to be sent to Treblinka was granted.

8 - My Sister Sonja is Dead

Shortly afterward, news spread of a forthcoming Juden Aktion. Some people fled to neighboring villages to hide. In most families nothing was discussed in advance, there was no time for that. Each person had to look after themselves. Our motto was: "Every man for himself!"

My sister Sonja, only three years older than me, ran to an acquaintance, the farmer Matynkowski in Zabikow and hid there. A Gendarme from Radzyn, who often passed our house and therefore probably knew my sister, happened to see her leaving her hideout and recognized her as a hidden Jew. Without asking a single question, he shot her on the spot. Today I would still be able to identify that Gendarme, because he was extremely short. My sister was 23 years old when she was buried in a roadside ditch. Although so many Jews were shot in the forests and fields, nobody dared to retrieve the corpses after the last incident. After the war I was finally able to collect the remains of Sonja through relatives and to bury her at the Jewish cemetery of Radzyn, which of course is no longer Jewish.

Originally we had considered Sonja fortunate because she was able to hide on a farm outside of Radzyn. But apparently fate had decided otherwise.

Sonja was a very pretty girl, good-natured and vivacious; she was brought up to love her home, her friends and Zion. The Zionist youth organization, Hashomer-Hatzair, was her second home. She hid because she loved life so much and wanted to live. An order for her arrest did not exist, nor did her death happen during an Aktion against Jews. Like an animal in the woods or a bird in the sky, she was shot arbitrarily. No report was written; no police and no prosecutors were called, no cemetery plot ordered, no grave dug, no stones placed according to Jewish custom, and no flowers scattered.

The murderer wore a grey-green uniform with a swastika on his chest and "God is with us" inscribed on his belt buckle.

What was happening to us Jews caused one to question God and the conscience of mankind. Was this the same almighty and compassionate God to whom we had been praying for thousands of years who let all this happen? Why, out of so many people, all of whom were under His protection, did some become killers, others victims?

That my parents had to experience such days was for them retribution from God. Contrary to the law of nature, according to which children usually survive their parents and bury them, my parents were compelled to mourn their children who had been torn away from them by murderers. After the son, the daughter. Our hearts were heavy. We hardly spoke with each other. There was nothing to talk about. A silent Kaddish on our lips and some tears were our farewell to my sister Sonja, 23 years old, lying somewhere covered with dirt in a ditch, killed only because she was a Jew.

It was the summer of 1942. The slaughtering of Jews continued unabated. The living were actually already dead, awaiting only the hour of execution. To withstand one's own suffering was difficult enough, but watching the pain of other family members was even worse.

Everyone was prepared to make any sacrifice in order to save a friend or a relative from suffering. Each one of us was willing to give up everything; there really was only one thing at stake for us – our lives. All else had already been taken from us. They confiscated our lives piece by piece to get the most satisfaction out of it.

Our fathers had to carry their children to their graves, men their wives, brothers their sisters and vice versa. The last Jew was to die just like the first. We knew that our end was near. To the last survivors were bequeathed the agony of separation and the mourning of relatives. This was a grievous privilege. In the time that was left to a survivor, regardless of how short, there always remained hope in God and justice, a vain belief in last-minute miracles.

The Nazi murderers cannot be compared with other killers. A comparison with other murderers and crimes of former or later times is a disparagement of the Nazis' victims. There has never been anything similar in history, and the 6 million victims are not alive to testify.

From my family there still remained: my father, my mother, my oldest sister Idessa, her husband and their 5-year-old child.

9 - The Judenrat

Under pressure from the Gestapo, the power of the Judenrat increased and it became more threatening. The purpose of the Judenrat was to help the Gestapo put their measures against the Jewish population into effect. The members of the Judenrat were not elected by the Jews, but were appointed by the Gestapo.

Because of their position, they were not as susceptible to hunger and abuse as their powerless fellow sufferers. The Judenrat tried again and again to assuage the Nazis by means of friendly words, gifts, and every kind of cooperation. For the members of the Judenrat, once committed to the task, there was no chance to withdraw. They sank increasingly deeper into the quagmire and became a tool of blind obedience to the Gestapo. On one hand they lived under the illusion of having more power and being better protected but on the other hand, they often had to submit to impossible orders. Carrying out the Nazi's orders, the members of the Judenrat justified their actions by claiming that if they did not help the Nazis, someone else would.

In retrospect, the members of the Judenrat, with few exceptions, should be pitied rather than condemned for their activities. They were partly responsible for the distribution of apartments, work, food rations etc. In addition to distributing food rations, they, in essence, also had to assign quotas of suffering among the Jewish population.

To comply with the commands and measures of the Gestapo, the Judenrat needed a lot of money. In order to extort most of these funds from the community, the Judenrat tried to prove its efficacy to its patrons by visibly securing releases from work, apartments, certain alleviations etc. Because of these advantages, some were favored while others were discriminated against. Of course, this procedure led to hatred and jealousy among us Jews, which was the intention of the Gestapo.

Thus, some people could buy their way out, or at least choose the kind of job they wanted. Again it was the poor, the refugees, who had to do the menial tasks and take risks just to survive. The situation became critical in light of the Endlösung as the Judenrat became an extension of the Gestapo in the liquidation of Jews. Out of pure egotism and an understandable selfish attachment to life, the Judenrat often became the tool and abettor of the Gestapo.

In the beginning of the resettlements, many Jews, and perhaps Judenrat members too, were credulous and naïve. But soon the truth about Treblinka became known. Despite this, the Judenrat continued to compile lists. With the help of these lists, they decided who would die sooner and who later. They played a treacherous game, probably the worst in the history of the Judenrat.

It was a vicious circle: one victim was supposed to extort from the next one and drive him to death. What was so strange and tragic about this process was that there was always someone willing to cooperate even though the same fate clearly awaited him. The Judenrat disbanded in Radzyn; most of the members disappeared or were transferred. The elder of the Jews stayed with his first assistant, Gruenblatt, who compiled the lists. As far as I can remember, Gruenblatt was still busy making lists even though at the end there were only 60-80 Jews left in the town.

The most inhuman order of all consisted of providing a number of Jewish people for extermination before a certain date. For Lichtenstein and Gruenblatt in Radzyn – and others in other cities – their punishment was the task of deciding who would die sooner than others. The first chosen for transfer were the mentally ill, the elderly, the invalids, those where were unable to work, and people, who in any case, did not have long to live. In this way they believed that they were playing the godlike role that the SS had assigned to them according to the rules of mundane justice. But in reality, God's order of things was abused in the implementation of the inhuman commands. Money, kinship, friendships and other relationships were the decisive factors in one's resettlement. Some judgments were postponed, but more were annulled.

It is no wonder that these two men who had the absolute power of life and death over the Jews of Radzyn were feared and hated by everyone. Nothing else was important anymore. This was true only for a short period, however, since their selection soon decreased. They had only themselves and perhaps their families to pick from, and soon not even that. So it was in our town and in all the towns where Jews lived and Nazis ruled.

10 - The Poles, the Germans, the Jews

As time passed we realized that it would be impossible to survive in Radzyn. In order to save themselves, many Jews went to villages and forests where they tried to establish contact with the partisans. Supposedly there were Russian prisoners of war and also Poles hiding in the woods. When the Gestapo noticed that many Jews had fled, they offered the Poles a reward of one kilogram of bacon and one of sugar for each Jew they turned in. After that, it often happened that Polish farmers caught a Jew, tied him to one of their flat wagons, and, like taking a pig to market, turned him over to the Gestapo for a reward.

Increasingly, Jews were found who had been stabbed, beaten, and robbed. For this reason, many Jews returned to the Jewish districts and ghettos with their spirits broken. Some tried their luck disguised as Poles, registering voluntarily as foreign workers; others tried to hide in the big cities. In all cases, we were dependent on the support of the Polish population whose assistance unfortunately was rare. To the contrary, the power of the Nazis was partly based on the considerable support which anti-Jewish laws received among the Polish population. It was not by chance that Poland was chosen as the place for the extermination of the Jews.

We Jewish people, above all the youth, knew enough about our situation and evaluated it correctly. We were all prepared to sacrifice our lives in the battle against the Nazis. We would have been glad to be able to offer resistance. It was not heroism; we simply had nothing more to lose. Unfortunately, there was no central organization to guide us. The whole Nazi machinery was organized and directed against Jews. We had no mail service, no use of telephones, trains, streetcars, buses, trucks, wagons, not even bicycles. Failure to obey meant the death penalty. A Jew without a Judenstern who happened to be among Poles was inevitably recognized, if not by the Germans, then by the Poles, and turned over to the Gestapo. A Jew could not leave his house or apartment for even five minutes without facing the danger of being detained by the Gestapo, the Schutzpolizei, secret agents or the Jewish militia. Each of these watchdogs could throw us in prison or make us shine shoes, clean toilets or perform any menial task they wished. They could send us to Auschwitz, Treblinka or Majdanek. There were also allowed to beat us to death and rob and shoot us; it was open season for Jew-hunting.

How many times did one meet someone in the street and planned to meet again only to find out the next morning that the person had disappeared? The Nazis sought to block all communication. They surprised us with their inhumanity at every turn. Their brutality was so incalculable that we could not conceive of any man capable of such behavior. Therefore we always reacted too late to avoid them.

At the German civilian and military offices of Radzyn, the expectations of victory began to vanish. The German Army's invasion of Russia could be well observed from Radzyn, which is only 70-80 kilometers from the border. One began to see more frequent convoys of wounded German soldiers returning from Russia. At the same time, one saw thousands of Russian prisoners of war. They were often guarded out in the open where they died en masse from malnutrition. Some managed to escape and hide in the woods, where they too died of exhaustion, disease and hunger.

11 - Uncle Jankiel and the Gypsy Woman

In spite of it all we continued to live. The flood of laws and decrees did not cease. Every Friday there were new ones and, in addition, death sentences in agreement with what had been decided at the Wannsee Conference. Every day local and German police or SS officials shot, arrested, assaulted and deported Jews. With true Jewish fatalism, we endured. Worse, there were the organized Aktionen. According to the Wannsee resolutions, they were called resettlements or penal Aktionen. The consequences were always the same and ended with deported, beaten, wounded and dead Jews. Such campaigns were considered particularly successful when they took us by surprise. These unexpected attacks usually took place at night or during the early morning hours. In the course of these Aktionen, apartments and houses were ransacked.

Once, when news of a forthcoming Action leaked, I went into hiding with my uncle, Jankiel Hochbaum, in a barn at the edge of town. My uncle was already old enough to be my grandfather. He was intelligent and enjoyed a good reputation. Although he fought hard for his existence, he was sustained by the memory of what he had been in the prime of his life. He was recognized as a learned man and had made his living as a sort of judge in arbitrations and by dispensing and selling eizes (advice). Along with that, he also made good use of his hobby, playing cards, to add to his daily income. Lichtenstein, the elder of the Jews, respected his sagacity to the extent where he protected him as long as he could. He had five sons all of whom were confirmed communists. At the beginning of the war they had run away to Russia. Because we rarely had contact with other members of the family, I knew very little about my uncle. During the time we spent together in hiding, I got to know him better and was inspired by his stories. He had a talent for recounting events from his life in an enthralling way. I was a good listener and spellbound.

I still remember one of these stories very well. Some years before the war started, shortly before May 1, one of his sons placed communist posters conspicuously on a wall. This was prohibited. One of the neighbors, the wife of a Polish policeman, happened to see him. Fulfilling her obligation as a good citizen, she reported the incident to the police and my cousin was arrested. An imprisonment of 3-5 years awaited him. My uncle, of course, found no peace; he had to free his son, but how? One day a gypsy appeared at the door of his apartment and offered her services as a fortuneteller. Since my uncle did not believe in this practice, he tried to get rid of her. But the gypsy, who wanted to earn some money, remained stubborn and insisted on showing off her powers. Finally he admitted her to his apartment. She told him all kinds of stories which went in one ear and out the other. He noticed, however, that she was a shrewd lady. Therefore, he told her about his detained son, who was awaiting sentencing for putting up communist posters. Soon they understood each other perfectly. The gypsy offered to tell the fortune of the policeman's wife using all of the necessary tricks, and my uncle provided her with full details about the policeman's family.

Shortly before the trial, the gypsy went to the woman's apartment while she was alone and offered to tell her fortune. Like my uncle, the woman resisted, but through cunning and deceit the gypsy managed to be let inside. First she told the woman everything about her family using the information my uncle had supplied her with. In astonishment the policeman's wife listened attentively and became increasingly respectful of the gypsy. Having gained the woman's trust completely, she was allowed to read her palm. "I see someone whose life depends on you. If he is saved, then there will be great good fortune for you. The disease from which you suffer will gradually be cured, your husband will be promoted and a happy marriage will await your only daughter. If, however, you contribute to the suffering or death of this person, then I see something terrible in store for you. Your sickness will become critical, your husband will receive an assignment that could be tragic for your family and I also see misfortune in your daughter's future."

The policeman's wife was impressed and knew immediately who and what were meant. A few weeks later the trial took place. The witness changed her statement, saying she was not sure anymore that it was my cousin who had put up the posters. Consequently, the accused was released due to lack of evidence. The gypsy had successfully completed her assignment and was paid accordingly. About two years later the gypsy's own fate was determined in Auschwitz.

The policeman's wife looked to the future with confidence. It was not the gypsy's fault that war broke out and that the policeman was not promoted. When the hostilities began, my cousin moved to the "red paradise" from whence he never returned. The fate of almost all Jews mirrored that of my uncle.

12 - We Make Plans

Our clique of friends, the Hevra, started meeting more often and devising plans. Our leader was my friend, Moschke Gellermann, who was somewhat older than me. He worked for the photographer Karlowicz. A girl from Warsaw, a Polish patriot, also worked there. She was touched by the fate of the Jews and wanted to help. Moschke's cousin, Saul Ackermann, a refugee from Danzig, was also in Radzyn. He had connections with a former Polish navy officer who had been expelled from Danzig and was at that time living in Bedlno near Radzyn. He and his wife were Polish patriots, friendly toward Jews and active in the Polish underground movement.

At about the same time Ojzer Ojzermann, our friend from the town of Miedzyrzec, came to Radzyn. He was also a member of the Hashomer-Hatzair organization. He told us about a youth and resistance group that was being organized in Warsaw and other cities and encouraged us to become active too. We were enthusiastic about his news but due to communication issues our efforts were hardly serious.

An estate, Suchowola Manor, which was 15 kilometers away and had once belonged to the Polish prince and anti-Semite Czetwertynski, was confiscated. It was said that the Germans had offered him a position as a sort of collaborator which he rejected, even though he had often organized pogroms against the Jews. The SS official Schulz took over the administration of the farm. Schulz soon became well known in the area for his terror and brutality. At the manor he built a camp in which he held Jews not only for work, but to satisfy his sadistic tendencies. The number of Jews in the camp depended on his mood. It was a one-man business. For his guest appearances at local Aktionen, Schulz always arrived on horse. When he was in Radzyn, the town belonged entirely to him. He killed and tortured and enjoyed the fear he inspired. He only rode to the places where the Jews lived and always on the sidewalk. Although everybody tried to hide he always found victims. He seemed to sniff them out like a dog, no matter where they were. At first he beat them, then he either let them go or took them along depending on his mood. His brutal appearance was in keeping with his "work"; he looked like the incarnation of a criminal record.

My best friend, Scholke Gellermann, with whom I had grown up, became a victim of Schulz and was taken to the Jewish slave camp at Suchowola. To his surprise, Scholke Gellermann found favor with Schulz and was named elder of the camp. Considering the situation, Scholke enjoyed a relatively good life there. At least he was safe from other persecution and deportation. Soon Scholke had his brother join him and together they became the managers of Schulz' camp in Suchowola. Shortly thereafter they brought their parents, friends and relatives to the camp as well. Idl Turkeltaub, Idessa Turkeltaub, Rochelle Nussbaum, Mosche Kaschemacher, Jachiel Leuchter, and Tova Elfenbaum and many more were among those who found temporary protection in Suchowola through the Gellermanns. They worked in the fields, had enough to eat and felt secure as so-called "useful" Jews.

Under the pretext of needing something from the town, the Gellermann brothers came to Radzyn almost every Sunday. The Hevra met with them at that time, usually at the Kamienistzkis' or at my home to discuss the situation. Together we came to the conclusion that we had no chance of surviving in Radzyn. We agreed that we did not want to die like our fellow sufferers had before us. We talked about the heroes of our past, Bar-Kochba and the Maccabees, and we dreamed of saving our people's honor. We were ashamed of the present.

Through the Gellermanns in Suchowola, we had more possibilities in Radzyn than before. We even had some weapons, although hardly anyone knew how to use them. A friend of ours from Warsaw, who had connections there, played an important part in our plans. We knew that there were several groups in the country with the will to survive, but meeting and organizing was almost impossible. Nevertheless, we had made a start. Thanks to some friends, we established connections with the Polish underground. Through our friend in Warsaw (whose name I unfortunately have forgotten) we maintained contact with the Hashomer-Hatzair headquarters.

In view of our hopeless situation and limited possibilities, we decided to procure forged Aryan papers, move to Warsaw and disappear in the big city. It did not take long before the Aryan papers, including birth and work certificates, were ready and waiting for us in Suchowola. The Polish photographer, who had worked with Moschke at Karlowicz's, was given our trust and she played an important part in the operation. She offered us her mother's apartment in Warsaw as a first contact address. The wife of the Polish naval officer from Danzig was willing to accompany us, two at a time, to the big city. There we were to live outside of the ghetto with Polish families from the underground. Of course, all expenses were to be paid by us. Hence, we decided to sell everything that we could not carry with us and converting our possessions into cash and valuables. We were twelve people, young boys and girls who happened to come together as a Hevra, but there were many more people waiting for such an opportunity of fleeing. For reasons of security, no team of two was to know the addresses of the others. Only Moschke and his Warsaw friend would know all the addresses and establish lines of communication among the different groups.

We really believed that we would be able to hide among the masses in Warsaw. It was a good feeling to imagine not dying on the orders of the SS. We were enthusiastic about joining the resistance and working with the underground. Today I realize that it was a childish and naïve idea to go to Warsaw, and that many people from Warsaw saw that their only chance of survival was in the provinces. Today I also know that several hundred Jews hid and survived in the dense forests near Parczew, which was only 40-60 kilometers from Radzyn.

The elder of the Jews, Lichtenstein, owned one of the town's most beautiful houses. When the Germans marched in, they confiscated his house and used it for the more prominent members of the occupation forces. The city councilor lived in that house as well as Brueckner and Mr. Moebius, both from Dresden, and other Gestapo families. One day it caught fire and was badly damaged.

Lichtenstein immediately arranged to have 40-50 Jewish specialists start rebuilding the house. Since the restoration was in the Germans' interest, Lichtenstein thought he could therefore save 50 more people by making them "useful" Jews. The Germans agreed; they did not have to pay the workers anyway. They rewarded these Jews simply by prolonging their lives, at least for the necessary working period, excluding them from the lists of those bound for Treblinka, if only temporarily...

I too went to work on the reconstruction of Lichtenstein's burned house and helped out in other German offices as well. But the important thing was that I kept myself under the wing of Simon Lichtenstein, the son of the elder of the Jews. My sister and brother-in-law, who lived with us in a tiny apartment, worked for a German company, Overbeck from Bremen. The company sold household goods and machines in exchange for coupons, for which the farmers had to deliver grain. Due to their work with this company my sister and brother-in-law received adequate food, and most importantly, they felt safe in their roles as truly useful Jews. Their German employer underpinned this belief. When the moment came, however, everything proved to be an illusion. The gentleman from Bremen let my brother-in-law and my sister down.

13 - The Transports to Auschwitz and Treblinka

In 1942 the machines of death were in full swing. Even the last optimists who had believed in survival gave up. Jews were transported from all cities and countries to Auschwitz and Treblinka. The Endlösung was no longer a secret. Everybody talked about death.

That direct transports no longer went from Radzyn to the extermination camp of Treblinka was attributed to Lichtenstein. The real reason was, however, that there were so few Jews left that it was not worthwhile to use trains. The Radzyn transports went only as far as Miedzyrzec, the closest regional collection point, and from there, on to Treblinka and Auschwitz.

Mr. Gruenblatt and Mr. Lichtenstein felt so protected that they no longer let themselves be influenced in composing lists. Only those who were extremely privileged and had something special to offer were allowed to see them. Gold and valuables had lost their power. Selection gradually became more difficult for Lichtenstein and Gruenblatt. The order of preference was the following: the elderly, the sick, those unable to work, dependents of workers, critics, complainers, and undesirables. The commodity called Jews was now in short supply. Still the machines of death would continue working as long as a single Jew was alive.

The resettlement of Jews from Radzyn to Miedzyrzec took place in the following manner: on the pre-arranged day, 50-100 or more peasants were ordered to appear early in the morning with their horse wagons at Szkolna Street in the Jewish district, where they formed a convoy. The Judenrat and the Jewish police called out the names of the Jews on the list. German and Polish police watched to make sure everything took place according to the rules. In the event of any minimal resistance directed against the Jewish police – which happened often enough – the Gestapo rushed in with pistols, which made the trip superfluous for that particular candidate. Patient and usually apathetic, the condemned took their few belongings, a pillow and a blanket, said a last goodbye to their relatives and took their place in the convoy. There were often heartbreaking scenes, with many families losing several members simultaneously. Those who stayed behind accompanied them, as if they had also been sentenced to the guillotine, knowing that it would soon be their turn.

None of the closely-guarded transports arrived without any dead – that was known. Soon into a trip to Miedzyrzec, which was 25 kilometers from Radzyn, a vehicle with Gestapo officials usually appeared. The Gestapo then shot arbitrarily at the line of wagons, killing 10 or 15 people each time. Shortly before arriving at Miedzyrzec, the convoy was welcomed by the police and SS in the same way, eliminating more people. The survivors who arrived in the ghetto of Miedzyrzec disappeared among the nameless and condemned and vegetated until they were sent to the Treblinka camp.

The trains to the extermination camps continued to depart and there was an increase in the number of young people jumping off moving trains and returning to the town. People knew that they were being driven to their death, so as soon as the first ones jumped, it became contagious, and some cars arrived half-empty. Unfortunately, many of the jumpers lost their lives, since SS officials would shoot from their hiding places. Many of those fleeing were hit; some were wounded and remained lying somewhere, those who escaped uninjured had to rely on the mercy of the Poles. Most of the train jumpers, whether wounded or uninjured, were robbed, killed or turned over to the Gestapo for a shameful bounty of one kilogram of sugar or bacon. We will never know how many Jews lost their lives on the tracks leading to Treblinka, Majdanek and Auschwitz because of the sins of others.

Very few of those who jumped returned to the ghettos. We did not dare to talk about them, because the Gestapo had informers everywhere. For that reason, we created a code word for jumping off trains: "Tralala". "Where did you come from?" "Tralala" meant I jumped.

Since it was important to all of us, we soon exchanged instruction in the art of jumping. The jump had to be in rhythm with the movement of the train and in the same direction, like diving into water. Landing only in soft ditches, never on bushes, trees or rocks, was recommended. An inside curve was not suitable, because it increased the danger of being shot by the SS. It was also advisable to carry a sharp knife with which the walls of the car could be slit open. Only in this way could one gain access to the bolt on the outside of the door.

14 - My Grandmother, the Bobeshi Basia-Gella

Much has been written about Jewish "mammas". Much less has been written about the Jewish "bobes" (grandmothers), even though they are known for their kindness and warmth. My Bobeshi Basia-Gella was for me a true representative of many Jewish bobes, a modest woman loved by all – and at the time almost seventy years old.

As a child, whenever I did something wrong or was afraid of my parents, I went to Bobeshi Basia-Gella. She was my lawyer, and always on the side of the defense. My bobeshi was very pious; she prayed every morning and evening and every Sabbath morning she went to the synagogue. In the afternoon she read Zeena-Reena – her only reading material – without making any mistakes, without omitting a word and always with the same mellifluous tone. There was hardly a sentence that she did not end with a sigh.

When she read, "Moses talked to the children of Israel and said…" or "Moses spoke to the children of Israel and explained," we tried to provoke her by asking what was the difference was between the verbs say, talk, speak, and explain. That often confused her, so she talked her way out of it all by saying: "That's the way it is written."

She was sure that Moses also received Zeena-Reena on Mount Sinai. Religion and family were her whole world and her life.

Politics did not interest her. For her, it did not matter if the Russians, Ukrainians or Poles governed. Pogroms, persecution and abuse were almost always the same for the Jews: why should things be different under the Germans? She believed that as a Jew, one was born to suffer and this would only change when the Messiah came. That he would come was never doubted by my bobeshi, or any other Jewish bobes for that matter. Why should they? First, it is so written; secondly, they prayed regularly on weekdays, and on every Sabbath they read Zeena-Reena without omitting a word.

Bobeshi Basia-Gella was for me a symbol of kindness and modesty, as well as a source of wisdom about life. Contrary to the Jewish men of that time who, in every conversation, flaunted their knowledge with quotations and comparisons from the Bible and were thus respected as learned, the bobes had to restrain themselves and be modest. Apparently, as women, they didn't count. However, conversations with my bobeshi were spiced with comparisons, proverbs and words of wisdom that derived neither from the Bible nor from any philosopher. Their origin was the experience of everyday life.

Some examples:

She would always say about two people who suited each other as partners, "Every pot has its lid."

About bad weather she would say, "Like in Jewish hearts" (i.e. that, because of the persecution, Jews were always sad).

If something did not take long: "The diaspora should only take so long!"

When talking about something good, she never forgot to add in Hebrew: "Without an evil eye."

Regarding something bad or evil: "May God protect and shield us, my children, your children and all Jewish children."

Referring to the dead: "May they rest in peace and be departed from us."

For the seriously ill: "May God protect us from hospitals and, as a precaution, also from prisons."

Additionally, she included people in her prayers in the following order: family, relatives, acquaintances, all the children of Israel in our town and our country, which then was expanded to include all good people in the world. She did not wish anything bad upon even our enemies and persecutors. This entire ritual she would finish with a "tfu, tfu, tfu, tfu, tfu, tfu", before spitting to the right, to the left, and in front.

In deep sorrow and desperation: "If that is how God wants it, then it certainly must be that way, because He sits up there and judges those down here."

When desperate: "You can just 'platz' (explode) from the way God runs the world."

No, she was not rebellious; not my bobeshi nor all the other Jewish bobes. The proverbs and general wisdom of that era are still valid and applicable today. I loved hearing her adages and have never been able to forget them.

When my Bobeshi Basia-Gella, who was one of the thousands of Jewish bobes placed on the death list by the Gestapo, was put on a wagon to be deported to Miedzyrzec and from there onto Treblinka, we could only think of one of her sayings and ask: "Can't you just 'platz' from the way God runs His world?" We asked ourselves whether she thought the same or, "If that is how God wants it, then it must certainly, or perhaps, be that way."

However, she did not say a word out loud, and with her head held high and without tears in her eyes, she climbed onto the wagon. Her gaze has stayed in my memory.

Together with several hundred Jews she went to her death that day. Upon arrival in Miedzyrzec, she was felled by the first bullet fired by the SS – the shooter was Heyn, who had made a name for himself as an eager marksman during transports. This is what befell my Bobeshi Basia-Gella, along with many other Jewish bobes. May they all rest in peace.

15 - Yom Kippur

Yom Kippur, 1942, the last one in Radzyn, was an unforgettable experience.

On this day of fasting and reconciliation, all Jews become very solemn and pray the whole day. It is the only day in our religion that is spent in fear of the Lord.

The elder of the Jews employed all his faculties and used his connections to enable us to pray on that day without being disturbed. He succeeded.

Without expressing it, everyone knew that this would be our last day of prayer, our last Yom Kippur, unless some miracle occurred. It was as if everyone wanted to reach God by imploring Him, screaming, crying, praying to Him, or breaking with Him, each one of us in his own way. It was a last attempt; perhaps He would help us after all. Otherwise it would be too late, for every last one of us. Our prayer on that Yom Kippur was the most emotional I have ever experienced. If there was ever one prayer, which could and should not be ignored in heaven, it was this one.

We prayed in a stable, near the store of the families Weidenbaum and Mandelbaum. About 40-50 men and women fasted, prayed and cried together. I cannot describe all the details; perhaps the author of Job could. Despite the promise of the Gestapo not to disturb our prayers, they came, ridiculed us and took some of us to work, wearing our prayer shawl and all. We cried. We cried not only tears, but blood, and poured out our hearts and souls in front of God. Out of the eternal prayer "Milehaim, Milamovet" ("Who is to live and who is to die") arose the desperate question: Why, why are we alone designated "Lamovet"? "Sqil srefa hereg veheneq" (from stoning, burning, killing or strangling). Is this the judgment and the kind of death that were determined for us, Your people, oh Lord, is this

Your decision, as to Your allegedly chosen people? Why? Why? Not only by the rivers of Babylon, but also here, here between the rivers Bug and Vistula, we sit and cry. Oh Lord, dear Lord, why did you forsake us? How can you watch what is happening to us?

When silence fell, it was the calm and quiet of death, though continually interrupted by sighs and sobs as if a knife being held to our ribs. People did not talk to each other. They really had nothing to say. Helplessly and powerlessly, we were merged by a common fate, each of us filled with the same thought: If our prayers are not heard this time and we get no help, then woe to us, woe, woe.

Levy Levi led the prayer on that day. He was a true Shliach-Zibur (messenger of the community) on that Yom Kippur. His heart-rending words were cries of pain from his soul and expressed the suffering of a tortured and desperate community. As our people have done for the past thousands of years, we wished and prayed that only the heavenly court, and no earthly judge or tribune, should determine our fate. We were unified as never before in a prayer for divine help against the cruelty on earth. All of us had the same wish, to save our very existence. Was that asking too much? Dripping sweat and shaking, we concentrated on the one vital question: will our prayers be heard this time?

Never before was our prayer "Al Heit, v'al Hatoim sheatanu" intoned with so much devotion. In the prayer "For My and Our Sins" (the literal translation) against God and man, one shows a commitment to these words through the Jewish custom of beating one's chest with each sentence. At the end of this section of prayer, God and man are asked for forgiveness and reconciliation.

If our affliction, we hoped that God, whose love and mercy we praised, would forgive us once again, protect us from further pain, and let us live.

Oh, how deeply did we feel our suffering on that last Yom Kippur! This was the pain which brought and held our people together, forged and unified us. We all had our personal tragedies while living the same hell.

When the prayer leader started to chant the prayer for the dead, "El-Moleh-Rahamim", (God the Merciful) and remembered all the murdered, burned and strangled men, women, children, fathers, mothers, sisters and brothers, the congregation choked on its tears. So few had to mourn for so many. The ones assembled here would soon belong to those who were cried over, with none left to say Kaddish for them. Ever since then, I think of this day whenever I say these prayers.

To ask me to describe all this is like asking a mute to speak. It is so hard to believe, understand and tolerate what happened and our experience of it. That is how the last Yom Kippur passed. Our prayers remained like a voice crying in the wilderness. Like always, we closed with the prayer "Leshana-habaa-b'Jerushalaim".

Nothing changed; it did not take but a year and it was not Jerusalem, it was Treblinka. Out of the group praying that Yom Kippur, I am the only one who happened to survive. We felt that, at least in this town and in this country, there was no more compassion, no pardon and no forgiveness, and that we could not escape from earthly injustice. Having tried to lean on God's love and to appeal for His justice, we felt rejected. The resettlements and deportations to Treblinka, Majdanek and Auschwitz continued. Those who still remained let themselves be lulled into a false sense of security by the Germans and the Judenrat. They put their trust in their being useful. Because we had to change apartments constantly, and because Radzyn was not a closed ghetto, we did not build any real bunkers or hiding places. In other towns and ghettos well-designed bunkers were built, enabling some Jews to survive one or two deportations.

In Radzyn, however, we were always taken by surprise and quickly delivered to the murderers.

Our daily life resembled a rudderless ship which floats aimlessly at sea without captain or destination. Abandoned by God and men, our distress signals were heard by no one as we drifted through storms encircled by bloodthirsty sharks. Across an already gray sky, new clouds gathered. One storm may be over but a hurricane was fast approaching.

16 - My Family, My Child

In the late summer of 1942 at about 4 a.m., we were taken unawares. The Jewish quarter was encircled by SS, Gendarmerie, Schutzpolizei, Polish police and by Ukrainian special forces (Sonderdienst), who we feared the most. Shots came from everywhere. People were beaten, houses plundered and demolished. They attacked us like vultures, grabbing Jews like predatory animals. Resignation was the only feeling left for the victims. On that morning 600-800 Jews were driven from their houses to one central point. Through loudspeakers the message came: "Anyone staying in their homes or hiding will be shot immediately. All Jews must report to the collection point!" Some families were given ten minutes to leave their houses. There was no way out. We waited while our fate was determined.

The usual routine began. Gestapo chief Fischer arrived with his entire staff and his dog. The elder of the Jews and his assistant, Gruenblatt, were standing close by with a list from which names were read. Each person called had to cross the street and take his place in the line. During those unbearably tense moments, we could not hear anything but the names being read. The judgment of the Yom Kippur prayer "Who is to live and who is to die" was pronounced by Gruenblatt in the name of the SS.

Soon we noticed, however, that those who were called had been selected to stay. We were experiencing a so-called "Selektion". About 70 names were read out. They were "working Jews", but the names of their wives, children, parents or other family members were not called. Only Lichtenstein and his assistant were allowed to keep their families with them. I was the only useful Jew in my family to be called. My mother, my father, my brother-in-law, my sister and their child remained. Up to the last second my sister and brother-in-law had wanted to trust their bosses from the Overbeck company of Bremen, who had often promised to help their loyal working Jews. But they had hoped in vain.

The ones driven together at the collection point were encircled by the SS and the police. Older people who could not walk were shot on the spot. Screaming women were beaten with rifle butts, and children standing in the way were shot. Only a few Jews had suitcases, blankets, or coats. Watching the moving lips of some, one knew that they were saying their last prayer.

When my family saw that I had been selected to stay, they gave the key to our apartment to my sister's child; she was supposed to bring it to me. It was probably a last attempt to rescue her, since the apartment was not really locked. In any case, she crossed the street with a smile on her face and came to me holding the key in her little hand. As though by a miracle no one stopped her. She handed me the key and I was able to hide her among the crowded rows of those chosen to remain. Thus she was saved, at least temporarily.

The time at the collection point was our last moment together. Each of us knew that the road to Treblinka led to the gas chambers. We looked into each other's eyes for the last time. There was no hysteria and hardly anyone cried; the pain seemed to silence our speech. Our quiet glances said everything. Some regarded it as God's punishment – perhaps that eased their pain.

Those who had been chosen to stay went home; the others were soon forced into trucks and taken to the extermination camp of Treblinka. Once again I had been kept alive, if one can call that living. That day marked the end of the Jews of Radzyn. It was also the end of my world. Like all others, I had lost my family, my beloved parents, my second and last sister and my brother-in-law.

Lonely, I stayed behind with a six-year-old girl at my side, "my child". How often have I reproached myself for not sharing my family's fate? Would it not have been just? What is God's justice? At that time I wished that the earth would open and swallow us all. I am sure that this was the hope of most of us. But alas, the earth did not open. I do not know where we got the strength to walk home. I took my last beloved family possession, my little Sara'le Süeßmann by the hand and we made our way home. Her small hand seemed to be secure in mine. We looked at each other without saying a word. I was 19 years old, the little girl barely six. In reality Sarah had aged more than I that day. Until then she had been a sweet, merry little child. Now she had stopped laughing. When I went to work in the morning, Sara'le insisted on accompanying me to the door of the office and waiting until she could not see me anymore. Five or six steps led to the entrance. Every day she came and waited for me on the steps that led to the office door during my lunch break at one o'clock. After lunch she accompanied me back to work and waited again until I disappeared from view. In the evening she was there on the steps again. It was the same every day, even in cold and rainy weather.

At home, too, Sara'le did not want to be apart from me; she even insisted on sleeping in the same bed. She fell asleep only by hugging me with all her child's might. I cried, but I didn't want her to notice.

She had lost not only the ability to laugh – she could not sing anymore either. She spoke softly and answered every question intelligently and to the point. But she said little. She never cried, played, complained, questioned, or asked for anything anymore; she was an entirely different girl.

I had seen and experienced many things during the last two years, but nothing shocked or depressed me more than what transpired these days and nights with my child Sara'le Süeßmann. Her eyes shone with a certain something that I can only cry about and not describe.

I did not have money or valuables. We lived off the food that remained at home. The few meals we had – if one can call them that – were always shared. It was a bit like a bird feeding its young mouth to mouth. Each of us wanted the other to have his or her fill first, so that they may live longer.

Sara'le transferred the love she had felt for her parents to me. Her feelings were an unusual mixture of sudden seriousness and a strong, childlike love, which both surprised and challenged me. As much as possible I played my role and tried to make her life easier. I would use up all my energy trying to cheer her up, distract her and play with her, unfortunately without much success. I may have been laughing on the outside, but within I was full of sorrow.

I realized that the child knew the entire truth; she knew that her parents had been deported and killed. She listened with indifference whenever I told her that her parents were on a trip and would soon return. Sara'le knew better. One could read her face like an open book. She knew that soon all of us, including herself, would be sent to Treblinka. But she did not believe that she would see her mother and father there.

She lived only for a short time, my child, only a few years, like almost all Jewish children during this period in history. In her suffering the plight of all of them was expressed. Whenever I see a picture of the thousands who answered the question asked by their Nazi propaganda minister of whether they wanted total war by bellowing "Jaaaa", I also see Sara'le against whom that total war was waged.

Against this unique "Child Holocaust", which can be found nowhere else in the history of mankind, no child raised his or her voice, nor pointed a finger, nor gave testimony, Anne Frank being a famous exception. Children may be victims, but generally not witnesses. Besides they are almost all dead.

I saw women suffering, heard men crying and witnessed the greatest agony of all – the agony of children. That is an anguish which cannot ever be forgotten.

Fortunately for both of us, my sister's sister-in-law soon joined us. She went into hiding during the big Aktion and escaped her tragic fate for at least some time. She took her niece in, and cared for her in the way that a woman can do so much better than a young man. I was very grateful to her for this.

17 - Alone in Radzyn

After these last surprising deportations, life in Radzyn never returned to normal. Instead it remained tense. Any belief in German promises had vanished. We became aware of the hopelessness of our existence. There was no complete Judenrat anymore, only Lichtenstein and Gruenblatt were still there. Jewish police and Jews who had worked for the Gestapo had also disappeared during the deportations. Jakob Ponczak and his friend Rosenzweig, who worked in the stables of the Gestapo, had been warned and therefore able, with great luck, to flee. They hid at the former mikva, the ritual bath. I lived nearby and provided them with food for several days until they disappeared and went underground. Ponczak survived the war and later died in Israel. Some of those who had been able to hide during the deportations reappeared, but it was not long before they were sent in convoys to Miedzyrzec. As I learned later, my child and her aunt were forced to join one of these transports.

In the town one soon started seeing rows of workers; this time they were not Jews, but Poles and Ukrainians. After the resettlements, the houses of Radzyner Jews were empty, and their apartments were picked clean. The synagogue was filled with furniture, household goods, clothing etc. The Wehrmacht who had been stationed there were long gone, along with their horses. Everything was sorted according to quality, but all the valuables had disappeared. They were sent home "ins Reich" or ended up on the black market. Some items were distributed among non-Jews or burned. For us 60 or 70 remaining Jews it was a traumatic experience to witness our own liquidation. For the Nazis and particularly the Polish anti-Semites it was a happy, long-awaited day.

At dusk we saw the shadows of people, probably Poles from the countryside, with sacks under their arms, on their way to loot. Those days belonged to delinquents and anti-Semites. "Hulliet, Hulliet (evil winds) – today is your time" was the apt way a Jewish song put it. It looked like the end – the end of a town, a people, a civilization or perhaps mankind. I do not know which; it was an end, in any case.

Our Hevra had more or less been spared by this Aktion. The Kamienetzkis' children and I stayed in Radzyn as useful Jews, but their mother had been sent to Miedzyrzec. The Gellermann brothers and a few others were in Suchowola. One weekend we met in my little house for the first time, which was more like a hut. Shortly before the deportations my family had been forced to move, so that I was living alone in an ugly wooden shack close to the mikva and other former Jewish public facilities. On some days the stench was intolerable. Nonetheless, the hovel was well situated on the edge of town, enabling us to leave at night without being seen. This fit in ideally with our plans.

We discussed the latest developments, agreeing that Day X was coming and that our only chance of survival – if there was one – was with forged Aryan papers. With these documents one could either disappear in a big city or go to Germany as a foreign worker. The latter was especially difficult, since it was forbidden for Jews to travel there. If one registered for transport with Aryan papers as a Pole, one was almost invariably recognized as a Jew by the Poles and handed over to the Gestapo. We thought it extremely risky to try to hide in the forests or villages. Many had tried and most had failed, ending up in the clutches of the Gestapo. Aryan papers were an absolute necessity for any attempt at escape. We all tried to get them. Preparations were made and the forged passports and documents were soon ready. We stayed together the entire night, eating a little and drinking vodka. The vodka was not imbibed for pleasure, but rather as a means to avoid thinking about what was to come, and what we had already left behind. Our Hevra still managed to talk for hours.

Those were hours of hesbon-hanefesh (soul searching). The counsels became a great moral support for all of us. We talked about a secret leaflet, good news about the war or successful acts of sabotage against the German military and extermination machinery, which was unfortunately still brutally strong and rather intact. We were happy about these things, but we knew that each of these activities amounted to no more than a mosquito bite in the grand scheme of things. Although we were disappointed and bitter, we encouraged each other and tried to not give up hope. Since almost every Hevra member had lost their family, we became an ersatz family united by a common struggle for survival. We were sentenced to remain together until death would part us. What little we owned belonged to us all. We lived in a commune in true harmony, willing to sacrifice all for one another.

Although we had dreamed of resistance in the past, of saving our people's honor, and of life after the war, we knew now, after the Wannsee death sentence, that a Jew could have only one goal, namely to save their own life and the life of any other Jew. With our new Polish identity cards we felt strengthened in our resolve, in spite of all the risks and dangers.

The will to survive often demanded an enormously high price, since it usually came with certain selfish instincts to which morality and humanity were sacrificed. Simply put, one's own survival was sometimes secured by placing others at risk.

The Nazi annihilation apparatus was based on an understanding of human weakness, egoism and amorality. For exactly these reasons, many Jews were faced with difficult moral dilemmas. Those untold persons who passed such tests and courageously faced their own deaths rather than endangering another human being belong among the most holy of people.

Many members of the Judenrat and the Jewish police were not thus holy. In their naiveté and weakness, they trusted the murderers and in essence became their accomplices. In order to save their own lives or make them bearable, they became blind and unscrupulous and forgot, overlooked and finally sacrificed their fellow sufferers.

I think that I owe it to my Hevra to stress that in this period of horror we never ceased helping each other to preserve our morals and humanity. Those values were my guide at this time.

The tension among the last 70 Jews in Radzyn did not vanish. News followed rumors in rapid succession. Word of another Aktion leaked out. We learned that only 25-30 of the remaining Jews would remain in Radzyn and even they would be imprisoned. This meant working under guard during the day and being brought back to the local prison at night. It would be a safe life, but without freedom and totally dependent on mercy – always fearing the Endlösung.

Until then we had worked at large, each of us having his own place to live. When this plan became known, our Hevra met again and we decided that we would not submit to imprisonment. We were not willing to be deceived again.

I had never talked to Simon, the son of the elder of the Jews and my protector, about our Hevra and our plans. I did not lack confidence in him, but members of the Judenrat and their families should not know about our plans, nor did they want to know. Because I did not intend to put up with imprisonment and told that to Simon quite frankly, he felt free and relieved. He had thought that I would ask him for help to avoid this fate. But for that even his connections would probably not have been enough.

There was never a dearth of surprises, about which one did often not know whether to laugh or cry. One such surprise was that Simon, subjecting to his father's wishes, was to marry Andzia Weinapfel before she was incarcerated. Miss Weinapfel was well educated and good looking. She only spoke Polish - albeit rarely and only to a few people. In every way she was a spoiled girl. She worked in the labor office (Arbeitsamt) and was regarded as useful and, because of her friendship with Simon, privileged. It is true that many young people married during the war, but that was when there was no Treblinka or Endlösung. Now that death was everywhere, the situation was different. Was it better to die married? A wedding and a honeymoon in prison? In my Hevra we really did not know what to think. It reminded us of scenes from the plays The Dybbuk or Joshe Kalb, where the wedding ceremony as well as the expulsion of the Dybbuk (ghost of a dead person) took place in a cemetery, since the country was now just one big, Jewish cemetery. I do not know whether the planned wedding actually took place. By that time, I had already disappeared with my friends.

Something strange happened to the two Kamienetzki sisters too. A Gestapo official, named Burger, in whose hands many Jews with Aryan papers had ended up, came to see them one day. They had once sewn clothes for him and his family, and now he warned them against procuring Aryan papers and trying to flee. Instead, he guaranteed to protect them for the duration of the war. But no one trusted Gestapo officials anymore. Moreover, all the preparations for the sisters' escape to Warsaw had been made. A few days later, they disappeared with the Hevra in the direction of Warsaw. Was Herr Burger brokenhearted? No one knew whether his intentions were good. As fate would have it, the sisters later fell into his hands again.

About 25 Jewish persons in Radzyn – the last of what had once been 5,000 – let themselves be voluntarily imprisoned. Not one of them survived.

18 - As Aryans in Warsaw

Our plan was to go and live in groups of two in Warsaw. None of us knew the addresses of the others. Only Moshke and his friend from Warsaw knew them and they were to act as contacts for all of us. This measure was necessary for our safety and had its advantages, but also disadvantages.

The day of our departure was approaching. I was not afraid, but my conscience did not let me rest. I did not want to save only my life, but also that of the small child for whom I was responsible. It was not easy for me to leave her, but there was no way to take her along. Staying in Radzyn would have meant death for both of us. Such a decision could drive a person insane. Finally, I clung to the thought – it was probably an excuse – of rescuing Sara'le by leaving her with a Polish family of the underground when I had established connections. With time she might forget the past and me as well.

My partner in hiding was to be Moshe Askereisen. He was about five years older than me. We belonged to the same Zionist organization and he had been a friend of my sister, Sonja. Shortly before the war he was drafted and managed to return safely. His three or four brothers had escaped to Russia, and his mother had been killed in an Aktion. She was wealthy and had had many friends among the Polish farmers, to whom she had given everything she owned for safekeeping. When her son returned, he could not reclaim his mother's possessions, since he didn't know the exact details. Hence, he was left to fend for himself. He lived with us until Day X.

One evening in November or early December of 1942, I locked the door to the hut, threw away the key and the armband with the Judenstern, and realized that I would never return to Radzyn. I did not say goodbye to anyone.

Moshe and I dressed as Aryans in high boots, riding pants, a short winter jacket and a hat with a feather. In our hands we carried small suitcases. We took side roads for six to eight kilometers to the village of Pludy. We stayed there for several days in a half-finished section of a wooden house. It belonged to a farm woman who was a friend of the Ackereisen family. The house was not heated and it was terribly cold. Winds blew through the cracks in the wooden walls. Everything in the room, including the beds and the bedding, belonged to the Ackereisen family. We were able to cover ourselves enough to prevent our freezing to death and were happy to have a roof over our heads.

Two days later the officer's wife from Danzig visited us from Bedlno. Elegant and beautiful, she instilled confidence with her friendly ways. According to my new Aryan identification card, my name was Jan Wozniak. My birth certificate and work permit bore the same name. We would repeat our new names and other vital information again and again so as not to make any mistakes. After discussing the final details and security measures, we set the date for our departure to Warsaw. To benefit from a cover of darkness, we chose a train that left Bedlno between 9 and 10 p.m. and arrived in Warsaw early the next morning. It was about three kilometers from our lodging in Bedlno to the somewhat remote train station. At a prearranged time we met our female companion, who gave us our train tickets. Despite the late departure, we passed several suspicious people who made us feel uneasy. As we boarded the train, we knew we had cleared the first obstacle.

The train was not full. For reasons of security we tried to change cars. Gendarmes, Polish police and train inspectors patrolled the train. They repeatedly checked individual passengers and arrested some. All of those people were Jews for whom there was no longer any hope of escape. I recognized some from Radzyn: Chancia Wolf, her brother and brother-in-law, Usiel Weissmann and some others.

We exchanged glances without talking but somehow understood each other.

I was talking with our guide, the officer's pretty wife, in whom I placed all my hope. My thoughts wandered to my abandoned child and my Hevra, some of whom were already in Warsaw and others who still had a long road ahead of them. Then I thought of all those who, unlike us, could not fight for their lives and therefore had to accept the death the Nazis prescribed. Hours of tension and uncertainty somehow always seem to last an infinity. In vain I tried to sleep, leaning on the officer's wife in order to hide my face. With closed eyes I saw and heard everything.

We finally arrived in Warsaw and left the train at Wilenski station. At the exit, innumerable German and Polish men in uniform and secret agents with their well-known leather coats, upright collars and hats pulled over their faces were standing in a line. Their keen eyes scrutinized every arriving passenger. They were all looking for the same commodity: Jewish blood. Our companion took our arms and after a few moments of terror we knew that we had succeeded. Half an hour later we were with the mother of the Polish girl photographer from Radzyn, who had given us the address. She was a poor, benevolent woman living alone. At her apartment I also met her son, who would later play a tragic role.

The mother and son lived in a small apartment on the ground floor in the back of a building. It would have been impossible to stay there. During the day it was dangerous because of the neighbors who, through windows and doors, could see everything. The place was crawling with informers. We lay down on the floor, the officer's wife between us, and waited for darkness. If I kissed her – I do not remember now – then it was only out of sheer gratitude.

Our friend Gellermann was already in Warsaw and had found accommodation for all of us through his connections in the underground. That evening our guide brought us to the new quarters where we said goodbye to that courageous and beautiful woman. We embraced and I kissed her in the hope of seeing her again. But I never did.

Everything had gone well so far. The feeling of being with decent Poles made us extremely happy. One should never lose faith in one's fellow man. The big jump had succeeded, but the struggle for survival continued.

Our new shelter in Warsaw was in Praga, Radzyminska 52, on the third floor with the Czeslaw Kidzinski family. He was a former circus acrobat with the stage name "Duo Alcaro", but at that time he was working for the railroad. Although both he and his wife, a cabaret dancer, were active in the underground, we never discussed their involvement, nor did we talk about Jews. Our room was furnished with two beds, two chairs and one small table. It had two windows but the curtains always had to be drawn. A picture on the wall showed a circus act featuring "Duo Alcaro". We occasionally left the apartment at night to get some fresh air. We always went out separately and were very careful, so as not be seen by the neighbors or the janitor. We were like two birds in a cage, waiting to hear from friends and longing for our Hevra and freedom.

After several days, our contact Moshke Gellermann came to see us. We were happy to hear that all of the Hevra had managed to arrive safely in Warsaw. Gellermann reported that our connections with both the Polish underground and with the Jewish Zionist youth organization, Hashomer-Hatzair, had been re-established. He also mentioned that the Ojsermann problem had been settled. This was the first we had heard of the Ojsermann problem.

Our friend Ojsermann from Miedzyrzec belonged to our organization and had connections with the headquarters in Warsaw. During our time with Hashomer-Hatzair, he had come to us and asked us to organize a resistance group. We did not succeed, since we were constantly exposed to persecution and Aktionen.

Sometime later, while the Gellermann brothers were still in Suchowola, Schulz, the notorious SS man, organized another Aktion in Miedzyrzec. Without saying anything to anyone, he went to Ojsermann's apartment and shot him on the spot. This murder bred suspicion in our Warsaw headquarters. How could such a thing happen when such a good relationship existed between the Gellermanns and Schulz? Why did Schulz go to Ojsermann of all people?

Moshke had been suspected of complicity; now it seemed he had been able to clarify the matter. To this day I don't know the details. Since none of my friends survived, I never found out anything more about this incident. There was so much hysteria then that this episode could have simply been due to carelessness or plain bad luck. I am sure, however, and will remain convinced until I die, that all the Hevra members, and especially the Gellermann brothers, were loyal friends, especially as they were fellow Jews and Zionists. They lived as such and as such they probably lost their lives in the Warsaw ghetto revolt. All honor to their memory.

During one of his next visits, Moshke told me how he had been recognized by so-called "Schmalzowniks". They were Poles who specialized in finding Jews to extort or turn them over to the Gestapo. They recognized him as a Jew and when he denied it, they dragged him into an alley where he was forced to pull down his pants. He was however, able to redeem himself for 10,000 zloty. This was our life in Warsaw.

Our costs increased constantly. We had to pay for lodging and everything else. The Kidzinskis were very decent Poles, but they were not purely idealistic, nor could we expect them to be. They were too poor for that.

Moshke and I paid a sum that should have been enough for all of us, and our money reserves should have lasted us a long time. Life with the Kidzinskis would have been easy if there had been no alcohol, and if our two Poles had not been so addicted to it. Every evening at six, when Czeslaw returned from work, the first liter-bottle of real or homemade vodka was opened and by ten o'clock it was empty. Everyone drank from glasses. I cannot remember ever seeing a half-full bottle there. In retrospect, I have to laugh about the first time I gulped down a glass of homemade "Bimber" vodka. It robbed me of both speech and breath. Only by raising my arms and being pounded on the back did I recover. We had to participate so as not to spoil their fun. After all, we depended on their mercy…

When Czeslaw's wife came home from the cabaret at ten o'clock everything started all over again, but this time there were four of us. As soon as we were drunk and our inhibitions had disappeared, the not-exactly-shy woman often began showing her feelings toward us, to which Czeslaw reacted with a show of real or feigned jealousy. Of course neither my friend nor I forgot our situation for a single moment. During the "high points" of such "Bimber" evenings, one had to be very cautious, since the danger of a confrontation grew steadily. Drunken people, particularly Poles, can be unpredictable. Polish drinking parties often end in fights, even among the best of friends. Fortunately this never happened for as long as I stayed there.

How to continue? Always the same question. We could not even think about the end of the war. In the underground, ideas circulated about the possibility of reaching Palestine by fleeing to Romania and from there to Turkey. But that called for money, lots of it. Nevertheless, people in our situation were enthusiastic about the idea. Our greatest asset was our access to stolen identification papers. People in the ghettos would have given anything to have these papers. To combine practicality and usefulness could mean our salvation. I discussed this plan with my friend Moshke and immediately saw that I could perhaps rescue my child this way. Full of enthusiasm, I volunteered to take forged Aryan identification cards into the ghetto in Miedzyrzec. This undertaking would be risky. But if it succeeded, my life would have meaning again, and my Hevra and my child, whom I loved more than anything in the world, would be helped.

It was the beginning of 1943. News of the war were encouraging but reports from the ghettos discouraging. In the Warsaw ghetto resistance was stirring. Outside, Jews in hiding were savagely hunted. Through Moshke we heard about everything that happened in the ghetto, including the preparations for a rebellion.

Everything now depended on the success of my journey to the Miedzyrzec Ghetto with fake passes. After my return something would have to happen. If the trip was successful, then we hoped at least to be in a financial position to fulfill our dream of fleeing to Palestine. The alternative was to join the partisan movement, but even for that one needed money. If I failed, only the ghetto remained. Holding out with Aryan papers was becoming increasingly difficult – almost hopeless. Seen from that angle, we all knew we had nothing to lose. We were actually gambling with lives that had already been lost.

We made all the necessary preparations. My escort was to be the brother of our Polish friend, the woman photographer from Radzyn. Of course he had been well paid. Neither Czeslaw nor his wife, or my Polish companion knew my real name. Even I had forgotten it. I was Jan Wozniak.

19 - Under Way with Forged Papers

On a Saturday evening in late February or early March of 1943, I said goodbye to my three friends, left the house and drove to the Wilenski railway station in Warsaw, wearing the same clothes in which I had arrived. A Jewish armband was sewn into my jacket, since I would need it to enter the ghetto. My Polish companion met me in front of the station. Again the military and civilian agents looking for Jews were everywhere. Once more I felt their attention directed toward me. Those parasites lived off our blood. Because the Germans were hardly able to recognize Jews shaved and in modern dress, denunciation and extortion were mostly Polish specialties. Hence we feared these Polish accusers more than anyone else.

Again I was lucky and got through. The train departed. This time I also did not feel any fear. The excitement helped me as a good medicine would. My spirits were raised. The weeks of hiding and endless waiting in fear and uncertainty, without being able to do anything, had crushed me psychologically. Now I was finally back in action; I felt that my destiny was in my own hands and I was betting everything I had against the Nazis. I almost felt like a hero. On the other hand, I tried to count the number of "death penalties" I had earned that day. The fingers of my both hands were not enough.

My companion and I were sitting in an open compartment, separated from each other. I had a small suitcase containing shirts, socks, etc., which was guaranteed to be "kosher". My companion had an old unobtrusive-looking bag, which was completely "trefa". This bag contained 60 blank identification cards, as well as 60 work permits and birth certificates, the necessary stamps, staples, ink and four other ID cards with pictures, signatures and accompanying documents. The four sets of documents which already completed were for four friends in Suchowola: Idl Turkeltaub, Idessa Turkeltaub and possibly the Gellermann's parents who were still hiding somewhere in the area. Moshke had told me about the four extra identification cards only moments before our departure. Those concerned were to contact me in order to pick up their papers. I was also to prepare and deliver an identification card for Eva Zyto. Eva was a very pretty girl and a friend from school; she could sing beautifully and all the boys were in love with her. In the end she had worked at the "Arbeitsamt" (labor office), and belonged to the half-privileged. When I arrived in the ghetto I discovered that she had been shot the day before because an Aryan identification card from another source had been found in her possession.

At about 2 a.m. we arrived in Miedzyrzec. Also in this station there was a line of Gendarmes, Polish police and secret agents intensely searching for Jews. We managed to get through and went to a nearby hotel. My behavior was self-confident – why and for what reason, I do not know. Perhaps it was because of my elegant clothes, the boots or the beautiful feather in my hat.

I presented a large banknote with my false identification card and was given a bed, as was my companion. I asked to be woken up at 6:15 a.m., emphasizing that I would be picked up at that time by a horse wagon from a neighboring farm, where I was working as an agriculturist. Should the wagon arrive earlier, I was to be roused immediately.

We were lodged in a room filled with beds in which mostly Wehrmacht soldiers were sleeping. We lay down, but I did not close my eyes throughout the entire night. Shortly before six o'clock I left the hotel, sneaked to the fence surrounding the ghetto and within an instant found myself inside. My Polish companion, who remained in the hotel, and I had arranged a meeting at 7:25 that same morning at a designated spot along the perimeter of the fence. He was to bring me the bag with the vital contents. If for some reason things did not work out, then a meeting at the same time and place was arranged for the next day. If we did not meet by the third day, then we would know that something extraordinary had happened.

Wearing my armband, I walked through the ghetto and found the house where my cousin Leo and other relatives were living. There I left my hat which was not suitable ghetto attire and could have attracted attention. I then hurried back to the prearranged spot along the fence in order to receive the bag. But my companion was nowhere to be seen. Feeling that I had almost reached my goal, the anxious minutes of waiting seemed like an eternity. The situation was not without danger since loitering near the fence was forbidden. Instead of my friend, a Gestapo official suddenly appeared. I knew him from Radzyn and was aware that he was now in charge of this ghetto. He shouted, "Hey, Jew, stop! What are you doing here near the fence?" Spontaneously I told him that I was supposed to work with the roofer and was waiting for him. Out of the corner of my eye I had spied a gate and a sign with the word "roofer". He slapped my face twice, nearly turning me around, called me a "pig Jew", grabbed his pistol and ordered me to put my hands up. I stood in front of him with my hands raised. He searched me from head to foot, opened my winter coat and my jacket, turned every pocket inside out, including the small watch pocket, and inspected every piece of paper he found. Fortunately, he forgot my back pants pocket. That was where I had stored the forged Aryan identification card, work permit and birth certificate in the name of Jan Wozniak. Again he insulted me with "pig Jew" and gave me a kick in the pants to speed up my disappearance. In my relief I hardly felt any pain, and I vanished immediately.

I regarded this event as a miracle and saw it as a sign that I would make it. I am usually not superstitious, but at that particular moment I was glad that I was.

If the Gestapo official had searched my back pocket and found my forged papers, he would either have shot me on the spot or taken me with him for interrogation. But I was still alive and felt even more encouraged.

The following morning I hurried to the fence again, but I was a few minutes late because a rude Jewish policeman had caught me, wanting to take me to work. I pleaded with him, but he would not release me. It took me a while to find a chance to escape. Out of breath, I arrived at the fence, but again my Polish escort was not there. I panicked, thinking that something unforeseen must have happened. As it was getting dark, I sneaked out of the ghetto with neither papers nor armband, which was punishable by death. I walked down all the streets around the hotel where we had stayed but could not see my friend anywhere. The next morning I was at the fence before the prearranged time. This time on the outside. Again he did not show up. I sensed trouble. Something must have gone wrong.

Now I was entirely on my own. We had planned to stay four to six days in the Miedzyrzec ghetto. Then we wanted to return to my first hideout, the farm at Pludy, which was about 20 kilometers from Miedzyrzec and from there return to Warsaw. For that reason, I had little money and clothing. We had only reckoned with two possibilities: either I would be caught while traveling or the mission would be successful and the papers would reach the ghetto. If I was arrested and tortured, there was not much I could tell the Nazis, since I had not been given any sensitive information before my departure. We had not even considered the third possibility, that after a successful journey I could lose contact with my companion. In such situations one cannot consider all the possible difficulties, otherwise one would not undertake any such endeavor. After three days, three nights and numerous stops at the fence outside the ghetto, I was unable to reestablish contact with my escort. I then realized that I was in an extraordinarily tricky situation. I felt like the ground was disappearing under my feet from one minute to the next.

With my cousin, Leo Schupack, I found a place to stay inside the ghetto. He was sharing his one-room apartment with his wife, his two children and my relative Miriam Blumenkopf with her two children. Miriam's husband had been a goldsmith and jeweler; he was wealthy and had worked for the Gestapo in his profession. When he saw the end approaching, he hid at a farm in a village. When his situation there became hopeless, he committed suicide by cutting his throat with a razor. There was nothing left for Miriam to do except return to the ghetto of Miedzyrzec with no money and her two children, a twelve-year-old girl and a younger son. Her daughter, Fradl, became the breadwinner of the family. She sold and distributed bread which she received through connections with the well-known baker, Leibisch. One day the girl caught a cold and developed pneumonia. Since there were no medical facilities in the ghetto, she died soon thereafter.

Two brothers who lived in the same room as Leo had been brought there from Parczew, a nearby town. They were about my age, but I had not met them before. Two or three Jews from Biala-Podlaska were also living with my cousin. One of them, Schepsyl Rosen (the only one whose name I remember), was a quiet, well-educated man. On New Year's Eve 1943, he and 50 other Jews were caught by the Gestapo and driven to a manure storage area on the edge of the Miedzyrzec ghetto. In celebration of the New Year, the drunken SS men shot them. They then ordered the Judenrat to remove the bodies. The Jewish police found Schepsyl alive but with several bullet wounds in his backside. Thus he was saved – temporarily. He originally came from Biala-Podlaska where, as far as I know, the Nazis committed their first big crime in the winter of 1939-40. They drove hundreds of Jewish prisoners of war and members of the Polish army of Jewish origin on foot from Parczew-Lubartow to Biala-Podlaska where their death march ended in a mass execution. In each town they passed through, several hundred Jewish prisoners were shot and buried in mass graves.

Thus, twelve people were already living in this small one-room apartment when I arrived. I was the thirteenth. Mrs. Gruenberg was the owner. She had a separate room, which she shared with her daughter and her twelve-year-old son. Her daughter and my cousin, Mayer Turkeltaub, disappeared one day before an Aktion, and found shelter on a farm. Later, in the seventies, they both died in Israel.

Only my cousin Leo knew the secret of my journey. On his advice we hid my Aryan papers in the attic. Thus I became a nameless Jew again, on his way to the Endlösung. It was understandable that I was not particularly welcome in my cousin's apartment. After all, I represented a certain danger for everyone, and I also needed food and a place to sleep, even though both of these commodities were scarce. Hence, I usually left the apartment before my cousins started to eat their small meals and returned when I was sure that they had finished. I appreciated the fact that Leo and the others always invited me to eat with them. I usually refused out of a sense of pride. They soon realized, however, that my claims that I had already eaten, were lies. Sometimes I did not eat for days, but my real anguish was the separation from my Hevra, which had become my second family, and my abortive mission.

Some of my friends and acquaintances from Radzyn were living in the ghetto of Miedzyrzec at that time. They knew about me and the Hevra. After seeing me in the ghetto in my miserable condition, they lost all respect for me. This was no time for sensitivity. Victors make history, but I was on the side of the losers.

20 - In the Ghetto of Miedzyrzec

Miedzyrzec was a collection point for Jews from a large area. In this ghetto in the center of the General Government, close to Treblinka, Sobibor, Belzec, Majdanek and Auschwitz, the Nazis put the Endlösung into effect. Here they could practice their sadistic methods as much as they wanted. It was a slaughterhouse that was filled anew as soon as the old stock was depleted. On average there where several thousand people living in the ghetto. Now there was no Judenrat, no administration, only a brutal Jewish police force that was known to cooperate with the Gestapo. There was no registration, no hygienic facilities, no fuel or other form of heating and no food. People lived on the reserves of their predecessors, if they could find any, or they would smuggle things in which usually entailed the involvement of the Jewish police. It was said that they would drink with the Polish police.

Every few weeks people were deported from Miedzyrzec, usually to Treblinka. The first task for arriving Jews was, therefore, to build bunkers and underground hide-outs. Thanks to these bunkers some Jews were sometimes able to avoid deportations and were saved, at least temporarily, from the camp.

Under these conditions disease was rampant. For example, my friend and relative, Schlomo Nussbaum, who was barely 20 years old, athletic and healthy, contracted tuberculosis and died shortly thereafter because there was no chance of medical treatment in the ghetto. Many people envied him because he was spared the ordeal of Treblinka. To die within one's own four walls was a privilege.

I met my child in the ghetto. She and I were happy to see each other again, but I had to listen to the reproaches of her aunt. Naturally I tried to defend myself and explain why I had left and what my intentions were, but I did not have much success. Although the child's condition had improved a little she never recovered from her depression.

Miedzyrzec was "Sodom and Gomorrah" for us. Everything there was more brutal and more violent than anywhere else. The Jewish police, including its agents and informers, distinguished itself by its brutality. This city during and after a "Judenaktion" reminded me of Bialik's book City of Slaughter. It was steeped in blood and in suffering.

An Aktion was like hunting wild animals. The police were the beaters and the SS the hunters. We Jews were chased out of our holes and hideouts into the open and then hunted like rabbits and foxes. This game was a pleasure for the members of the master race, who behaved like the wildest of beasts, lived in the greatest of luxury and were well fed and well dressed. They were well armed and demonstrated their strength and power by shooting the weak, defenseless, and broken men, women and children. The extent of their barbarity and sadism defied imagination.

In addition to one's own suffering, the crying voices of the hunted men, women and children, like the laughing and shouting of the murderers, frazzled our nerves. Each shot hit – if not physically, then morally – a Jewish soul.

After each Aktion the ghetto looked like a battlefield. The streets were filled with wooden blocks, iron bars, bottles, glasses, straw sacks, cans, toys, baby carriages and mattresses. Here was a pool of blood, there a pool of milk, paint or marmalade. One saw spilled flour, salt, clothes of all kinds, tallits, tefilin, books, shoes, hats, dolls, blankets and wheelbarrows. Here lay a man's or a woman's corpse, there a dead cat or rat and, out of their minds with fear, people ran back and forth. Bricks were torn out of buildings, stones out of the streets, blood, urine, excrement and trash were everywhere; everything stank. This was a hellish chaos – a total eclipse of humanity. Human dignity was trampled underfoot.

In the streets and gutters, torn and trampled books and pages could be seen. Especially noticeable beside the yellowed pages of the five books of the Torah were the oversized pages of the Gemorah and Talmud commentaries, including the leather covers in which they were formerly bound.

The pages of the Chumash and Talmud commentaries were highly respected by Jews. They were regarded as a symbol of scholarship and treasured as family heirlooms handed down from one generation to the next. When a page became worn out, it was buried like a human being, with care and respect. If a page fell to the ground, it was gently picked up and kissed. These books and commentaries, which were an early source of ethics and an inspiration for many religions, were now, according to the Nazis, the cause of all evil? Did the Aryan world, especially the "master race", now need to be freed of them?

In the history of mankind, there have always been brutal men, murderers and sadists, but never before has there been such organized torture. Someone who did not live through that period cannot imagine the reality and the extent of the Nazi genocide. The perpetrators of this crime dehumanized themselves.

For us it started with a naïve belief in the goodness of humanity, its culture and civilization. It ended in the death of six million Jewish men, women and children whose only crime was being born Jewish.

After these Aktionen, one saw those who had managed to survive crawling out of their hiding places, hungry, thirsty, bloody, with few of their human features still recognizable. They emerged with deeply sunken eyes, full of apathy, but occasionally also full of spite and hope. That is exactly what the Nazis wanted us to become. I was now living in the ghetto and, despite my hidden Aryan papers, I was convinced that I too would soon look like the others unless a miracle occurred.

After I had given up all hope of successfully completing my mission and realized that there was no possibility of acquiring the forged papers from my Polish escort, I began looking for information about his fate. I heard that a friend of mine from Parczew had been arrested for possession of illegal documents but had been set free through connections, and was now living in the ghetto. I went to see him to hear the details of his stay in prison and see if I could get some information about friends we had in common. He told me that the prison population was almost exclusively Jewish.

One day, however, a Pole from Warsaw was thrown into his cell; he had been caught with 60 Aryan identification cards and equipment for forging additional papers. The Nazis wanted to know who had commissioned him. He said that it was a "small, black Janek" who had given him 1,000 zloty for bringing a bag from Warsaw to Miedzyrzec in which he did not even bother looking. Janek was supposed to have entered the ghetto. I knew immediately who he meant since all the dates and the story of the 1,000 zloty were also correct. I had to exercise great self-control so as not to show too much interest. I heard the rest of his story as from a great distance. He added that the Pole was tortured repeatedly because the Gestapo believed that he did not want to reveal his employer. In the evening the Pole was led through the ghetto by the Gestapo and Jewish police in civilian clothes in the hope that he would recognize the "little Janek". My friend also told me that the Pole was still in prison at the time of his own release. The interrogation and the search for "Janek" continued. I fell into a mood of resignation and deep despair. After having escaped from Radzyn with great luck, successfully playing "cat and mouse" with the murderers, and having lived as a relatively free man, I was again standing alone and abandoned, helpless and discouraged as a ghetto Jew in the waiting room to Treblinka. I had no one with whom I could discuss my situation.

None of the persecuted here had time or patience for others. Each one fought his individual war against the strong and brutal military extermination apparatus. It was as if the fate and future of the master race depended on it.

With my Hevra, I had risked everything. Now, as a lonely loser, I had lost everything: my Hevra, my power and my last possibility to resist. The thought of being sought by the Gestapo and the Jewish police and that I might be caught at any moment…the torture that awaited me…the confrontation with my good, respectable Polish companion…How could I look him in the eye after having caused him to suffer so much? My main concern, however, was whether I would be strong enough not to betray my Hevra. Would I withstand the torture, or would I die in shame as a traitor?

In those days of discouragement, I considered it a punishment to still be alive. I regretted not having died anonymously with my family. Now I had the privilege of being broken first on a Gestapo torture table, with a name and as a known person.

I remembered an old saying of my grandmother: "When God gives tzores, He also provides the power to withstand them." That was my hope. Despite my apathy, however, I knew that I had to hide or escape immediately and since I could not escape, I decided to hide.

I hid in the bunker of my cousin's house lest I be recognized if the Gestapo and the Jewish police searched the house. No one was to know my whereabouts. Before I arrived, Leo and some boys had built an excellent bunker for 20-25 people. It was the secret of the house. The entrance was its most ingenious part: an outhouse in the backyard which could be reached quickly through an apartment window. It looked like any other lavatory with water and no sewage.

It was intentionally kept disgustingly dirty. The filth was our security. The cover could be opened by a trick so that one could climb down into a pipe which was supported by wooden beams. After 10-20 meters of pipe, one came to a room which was approximately two meters high and two and a half to three meters in length. The room was also supported by beams. In the center of the room was a barrel of water which was covered by a wooden board and this served as a table. There was also a bench with some blankets on which one could lie down.

I spent five or six days in the bunker and there I buried my dreams and hopes of emigrating to Palestine, reaching the partisans in the woods, rescuing little Sarah or going to Warsaw to meet my Hevra and again seeing all that which I loved, treasured and missed. I later received a terrible blow when I heard that the Gestapo, by means of the identification cards in my companion's bag, found the four young people in Suchowola, ordered a roll call of all workers, called the names of those who were implicated and shot them on the spot. They had waited impatiently for those papers and saw them as their last hope for survival.

Because of my unsuccessful mission, I felt that I was their gravedigger. Even today that memory still weighs heavily upon me. That these four identification cards were issued exclusively by Moshke Gellermann, and without my knowledge, was no consolation. Among those shot were Idl and Idessa Turkeltaub; I have unfortunately forgotten the names of the others.

The unhygienic conditions in the ghetto soon had terrible consequences. Perhaps we should not have been surprised when typhus started to spread. There was neither soap nor facilities for washing. Everyone in the house became infected except Leo. Although he cared for the sick, he never contracted the disease. Even before falling ill, I had been half-starved. Now we were suddenly three young men in one bed suffering from typhus. There was neither food nor medicine. Our "Doctor" Herskowicz was a refugee from Czechoslovakia and probably still only a premed student. His effectiveness was limited to the possession of a thermometer which always showed our temperatures to be over 104 degrees. Without proper care, food or liquids, we started losing our hair and strength and had to stay in bed. More dead than alive, delirious with fever, the three of us, hardly twenty years old, fought for our lives. But at least we were safe from Aktionen and the Gestapo who were still looking for me. The ghetto was given a respite. Signs reading "Typhus epidemic – danger of infection – entrance prohibited" could be seen on windows and doors. The Gestapo stayed far away. Supposedly 95% of the Jews in the ghetto were sick, but only 5% died, which is a miracle under such circumstances.

On one of those days during my illness, as if through frosted glass, I recognized Tova Elfenbaum from the Hevra in front of me. My friends knew that my mission had failed; they wanted to help me and get me out of the ghetto. For this reason, Tovale had come from Warsaw, for this she had risked the death penalty. She saw my pathetic condition, talked to Leo, and stood by my bedside for a few minutes, since she could neither talk to me nor take me with her. The feeling of not being forgotten by my friends later instilled in me a new will to survive.

Tovale Elfenbaum belonged to the younger generation of the Hashomer-Hatzair organization. Through the efforts of the Gellermann brothers, she, along with Moschke Kaschenmacher and Jechiel Leuchter, came to us in Warsaw when they were about eighteen. Almost all of their parents and relatives had already been liquidated, but they wanted to survive and were prepared to sacrifice their young lives to attain that goal. The entire Hevra, especially Moschke, had only one aim: to defend themselves and to establish resistance. For that reason, they tried to get more friends out of the ghetto and bring them to Warsaw without regard to their own safety, knowing that increasing the group meant a greater danger of being discovered.

All these young people who were imbued with Jewish culture, a love of Zion and were inspired by the idea of fighting against the Nazi murderers – all of them died nameless, and without graves.

I gradually regained my strength. Hunger was my main problem. Those around me also similarly suffered. I was so weak that I could hardly stand and keep my balance. When I buttoned my shirt, I broke into a cold sweat. In this condition, how was I to find something to eat? Or work? But with each passing day I grew stronger.

There was only one place where one could always find employment: the Gendarmerie or the Schutzpolizei of Miedzyrzec. The 30-40 Jews who worked for them were forced to do so, and their lives were in constant danger. A terror for all of us was a policeman of German-Czech origin whom we called "Der Schläger" ("the Beater"). He was a sadist who tortured and shot a few Jews at breakfast and lunch on a daily basis. Because of him, nobody wanted to work for the police. However, I volunteered.

We had to march in lines to our place of employment, which was about 30 minutes from the ghetto. There we were given all kinds of dirty jobs. On the first or second day, an officer arrived with a defective lamp and asked who could repair it. I volunteered, satisfactorily completed the task and was then given several similar jobs through which I attained a sort of special position. Although the work was paid for by the Judenrat, occasionally we were fortunate enough to find something to eat. Usually it was food that had been thrown away for not being good enough for the chickens or geese.

The officer provided me with work. One day he took me to the meat room where all kinds of meats were stored for the police unit. He ordered me to perform some electrical work there and locked the iron door as he left. In the frigid rooms were vats full of bacon and meats of every kind. Ham and sausages hung from the ceiling. Almost starving and only recently recovered from typhus, I felt like someone dying of thirst in the desert that finds a spring but is not allowed to drink. My stomach rebelled, but I was afraid to even taste anything. I ate with my eyes, but it was like licking sugar through a window. It was a battle between hunger and fear. Which was stronger? Although my hunger increased, behind my fear was the matter of life and survival. I thought that everything in the room must be accounted for. I did not dare take anything lest I be caught at the control point. An immediate death by shooting would be the inevitable consequence. So I decided to at first only rearrange the ham and sides of bacon. It was possible that the meats had been counted and that it all has been set up as a trap for me. I did that for two days, changing from morning to lunch and from lunch to evening. Nothing happened. On the third day I ate my fill for the first time in two or three months. During the next few days I ate once more and in the evening smuggled one or two sides of bacon into the ghetto in my waistband. After that I did not return to this job. The sides of bacon were my startup capital and gave me new courage and motivation. I was still alive and even full.

After the typhus epidemic had run its course, the deportation Aktionen continued in the usual manner. Some SS men in small groups carried out their own attacks in the ghetto. During one such midnight raid, I ran barefoot through the back of the house wearing only my underwear, and hid with others on the tin roof of an adjoining house. It was extremely cold. The tin sparkled with frost. We had to lie down on the roof so as not to be discovered. Our bare feet and entire bodies stuck to the cold tin. Every time we moved it felt as if our skin was part of the tin. At another time, out of fear for an announced Aktion, I fled with a group of people to a forest ten kilometers away. The woods were always considered a possible place of safety, but many Jews lost their lives attempting to contact the isolated groups of Russian partisans or others. Later, as the luck turned in the war, it became easier to disappear in the woods and to join the partisans.

Only with weapons did one gain the respect of others in the forests, and that was one of our chief difficulties there. None of us knew how to handle a weapon.

Upon arriving in the woods, we started to build an underground hiding place. Soon Polish foresters appeared and, without any reaction or movement, observed everything. From the looks on their faces we soon realized that in digging a hideout we were actually digging our own graves.

Without exchanging a single word, the foresters watched us quietly. Their faces revealed their intentions. Apparently they could not decide whether to rob us themselves or to turn us over to the Gestapo for the usual bounty. In any case, what awaited us was clear. We therefore decided to leave the woods before it was too late. Disappointed and in despair, we returned to the Miedzyrzec ghetto.

21 - The Ghetto is Liquidated

One night toward the end of April in 1943, we were awakened by the sound of gunshots. Although we anticipated Aktionen at any time, we were surprised. Everyone in the apartment hurried to our bunker. We took some of the neighbors along, since they knew about our hiding place and could pose a danger to us if they were left outside. The bunker was therefore overcrowded. The ghetto was surrounded. We heard the sounds of exploding grenades, wild gunfire, the barking of dogs, breaking windows, cries and screams of Jews, commands being shouted and spiked boots marching. Walls were torn down; iron bars and beams knocked down walls, floors and ceilings. We were like sardines, crushed together in the hot, sticky air of the small room. Soon everyone was thirsty and sweated from fear; children cried and wanted to relieve themselves. Parents pressed their hands tighter over the mouths of their children when they heard boots approaching. Every house was searched thoroughly. While looking for us, the Nazis looted. They stole textiles, leather and jewelry, hidden between walls and in the bunkers.

About 25 men, women and children were in our bunker. We repeatedly heard the command: "Give up, leave the bunkers!" This was accompanied by the sound of exploding hand grenades and gunfire. Between five and six o'clock in the morning they searched our house for the first time. We heard the noise of walls, doors, windows, and cupboards being torn down and a ram battering the walls to repeated commands of "Hau-Ruck". Everyone realized the seriousness of the situation. A movement, a cough or the slightest noise could have meant death for all of us. The deadly silence in the bunker was sustained with our final reserves of energy. I no longer remember whether it was 20 or 30 hours that we spent in that state, with dry throats, being pressed against each other.

I am convinced that no person who had a choice would opt for such torture even if the other option was losing his life. Once in such a situation, however, the will to survive seems to grow stronger. I discovered that not only in me, but in many of my fellow sufferers. We knew what awaited us but we resisted – more out of instinct than logic.

Our tormentors approached us in groups of four or six and at short intervals. We heard them shouting orders and pounding on the walls and ceilings. Then they disappeared again with their booty of people and goods. The occasional moments of silence were broken by screams and heartbreaking sobs and the whistle of isolated gunshots.

In the bunker, we were completely exhausted. The air was asphyxiating; the stench of sweat, excrement and urine was everywhere and we could hardly breathe. The three or four children in the bunker behaved like adults. They did not say a word, did not cough, cry or complain. They acted with the instinct of little animals. We hoped that this Aktion would stop and that the SS would disappear. We could then leave the bunker as we had done after previous Aktionen, which had never lasted so long.

We had been in the bunker for two days and two nights when we heard a new wave of attacks on our house. Again, they were in the house, above us and in the courtyard. This time it was more serious. They came in a group with crow bars and battering rams. Our persecutors knew from experience that the bunkers were not located in cellars directly under the houses, but on the sides. Cellar bunkers were easy to find because of the hollow sound they made when tapped. They therefore pounded the outer walls of houses until they heard a hollow sound. They rammed the walls near our heads until they finally hit the upper corner of our bunker. Fortunately they hit only the corner. The ram brushed it and penetrated the sidewall. Thus they could not detect a hollow spot. A deathly silence prevailed in the bunker and it was completely dark. The sound of the battering ram could be heard above our heads. Breathlessly we sat there, only seconds and centimeters from the killers. More and more dust fell from the ceiling onto our head; that was not a good sign. Perhaps we would suffocate before being discovered. Any end was preferable to this torture.

Suddenly a loose block of wood brought a ray of light into the darkness of the bunker. The murderers did not notice anything. The men and women sitting in the corner moved their heads to let the ram be driven into the wall. They then covered the corner with a blanket in order to prevent the light from revealing our presence. It took about 30-40 minutes before the persecutors gave up. They pulled out the ram and we filled up the hole with clothes to stop the light from entering.

Just when we thought that the search was over, the Nazis reappeared, this time at the toilet entrance to our bunker, which we had considered absolutely safe. Later we learned that they had discovered a neighboring bunker and were given the location of our hideout by a young man who knew about it. Under the threat of smoking us out with grenades, they ordered us to leave the bunker immediately. In such a moment there is neither the time nor the possibility for discussion. It was enough for one person to weaken and stick his head out. One of my typhus-infected comrades was close to collapsing; he panicked and emerged first. A bullet smashed his leg.

We crept out of the bunker with raised hands. We had spent two and a half days there were herded, with bayonets, into the marketplace. In 1947, in Marburg an der Lahn, I recognized the man who had revealed our hiding place. I found no reason to reproach him, but I did not want to talk with him either.

On the morning of April 30, 1943, my birthday, I fell into the clutches of our murderers. Several hundred men, women and children were rounded up and many more joined us. We were forced to sit on the ground with our hands over our heads. It was the end of all our dreams and illusions. Death seemed to come closer – death by gas, shooting or torture? There was no way out and no possibility of escape. That I had managed to save myself until then was of little consolation.

At the collection point I could see many acquaintances from Radzyn. I also saw my child with her aunt and uncle. Apparently all Jews had been caught during the raid. The ghetto was to be destroyed and all the Jews liquidated. Terrible scenes took place. Most people sat there apathetically for hours, others had already been shot. Children cried; mothers, who tried to console them, thereby attracting attention, were worked over with rifle butts.

Some people were randomly chosen and ordered to reveal bunkers that had not yet been found. If they said nothing they were beaten. When a woman became hysterical, a guard pressed a pistol against her back and fired. Confessions were extorted. Was our bunker also betrayed in this way?

As we lined up in rows of five, the Nazis noticed that some children without parents remained in the marketplace. They were probably lost in the chaos or their parents had been shot. The SS men would hold their pistols against the children's necks and fire. Endlösung.

In the afternoon we were led through the city to the train station. How the ghetto looked and how we felt have already been described. Outside the ghetto the world looked normal – almost normal. In my eyes the people also looked that way. I did not see a sign of compassion in the Poles' faces. They knew that the possessions given to them for safekeeping had become their own property forever and that when we marched any remaining debts could be regarded as settled.

Many Jews grasped each other's hands tightly so as not to be lost. There were men and women, sisters and brothers, friends, lovers, sons and daughters who did not want to leave their feeble parents in their hour of need. Small children in the arms of their mothers, who clasped them to their chests. One often heard muted crying, then shots and silence.

In great disarray, accompanied by shouted commands, we were beaten and shoved by rifle butts into waiting cattle cars. Families and friends were mercilessly torn from each other. Those who managed to stay together felt like they had won. Dogs were let loose to bite us and tear our clothing to shreds.

The doors were locked behind us and bolted. The small windows in the cars were covered with barbed wire. Through them, however, we got some fresh air and light. We could breathe and calm ourselves. We felt that we were at least safe from rifles and dogs. We soon became aware of our hunger, thirst and other basic human needs. All those people had suffered twenty or more hours of unimaginable torture – hours that seemed endless and which did not allow for attending to any need.

Occasionally a member of the Judenrat or the Jewish militia was discovered. Only days or hours before he had been serving our tormentors, but now he too had become a victim and shared the tragic fate of all Jews. Passively and silently they endured the curses, the spitting and the blows of their fellow sufferers. What could they have been thinking at that time? One must be thankful for having been spared such ordeals.

A few hours passed before the train got going. Some young men had knives and chisels. The cutting started immediately. About two hours after departure, a hole in the car wall had been opened, so wide that one could lift the bolt on the outside and slide the door open. In the meantime, night had come. The rattle of the train could be heard along with the shots of the guards who sat in booths between the cars. When the train moved slowly, the shots fell along the ditches, but always closer to the car doors. Operation "Tralala" – jumping off trains – had begun. Many people leaped, many died. I too wanted to jump. It was difficult to decide. I knew that I was the last survivor of my family, that I had lost my child and my Hevra and that I was one of the last of the 60 Jews from Radzyn. In that dilemma, I spoke with my cousin, Miriam Blumenkopf. She was much older than I and physically could not jump from the train. Her thirteen-year-old daughter had already died in the ghetto. I asked her if she could tell me where she had hidden some valuables so that I would have some money if my leap for freedom succeeded. Her husband had been a rich jeweler and had hidden or entrusted many valuables to Polish families for safekeeping. She rejected my request. I was neither angry nor offended; she had probably not understood the situation yet.

I do not know how many people jumped from the train that night, but it must have been a good number, since the shooting never stopped. Our crowded car was almost half empty when we arrived. I also do not know how many were shot and how many survived; I never met one of the "jumpers". However, I did not jump. We knew that our train was bound for an extermination camp, but we did not know which one. Would it be Treblinka, Auschwitz or Majdanek? Early the next morning we got our answer when we arrived at Majdanek.

22 - In Majdanek

The SS men welcomed us with their bellowing. They drove us out of the cars with rifle butts, yelling: "Get out, you Jewish pigs, you sows!" Men were pushed to the right side, women and children to the left. I took one last glance at my child before she disappeared in the crowd of women and children.

My first look at the prisoners was horrifying. Almost all of them had sycosis, which I had never seen before. Their faces looked as if they had been smeared with cheap brown paint. Some of them wore striped prison uniforms, others were dressed in civilian clothes that were black with blue and red stripes on their backs.

This was a completely new world for me – a world in which every word was shouted or screamed instead of spoken. We were ordered to undress. All possessions were taken from us. We were led to a big bathroom. Every possible human hiding place was checked, our heads were shaved and we received the striped clothes, striped caps and Dutch wooden shoes. We were not registered, but each of us was given a number with his clothes. My number was 1377. I realized that my name was being crossed off the list of mankind. My name was no longer needed nor would it be used; it could be forgotten.

Majdanek was only 70 kilometers away from Radzyn. The region was known for its fertile black soil. For me, however, it was a kind of Sahara. All of Majdanek was yellow sand. Marching in wooden shoes, to the accompaniment of the shouts of the SS guards, was very difficult. After marching 3 or 4 kilometers we reached Field 4 of Majdanek. There were four fields for men and an adjoining field for women. The whole area was enclosed by barbed wire and each individual field was encircled by an electric fence that was guarded. About 10,000 people worked in a field and each field contained several large barracks, so-called blocks. I landed in Block 24.

Majdanek was a torture and extermination camp. The prisoners were not assigned practical work, with the exception of a very few who were assigned administrative jobs.

The indescribably painful roll call which took place every morning lasted several hours. Many were nearly beaten to death. They could be sure they would not be part of the evening roll call. Then we went to "work", which meant we were forced to run in our wooden shoes to one corner of the field where we filled our caps or the corner of our jackets either with wet sand, stone or mud. From there we ran to another corner, emptied the mud, replaced it with something new and so on. Lines of SS officials and so-called prominent prisoners, equipped with clubs and whips, beat us along the way. It was hell. As a result of the beatings and exertion, many died or were injured. By orders of the kapos and the SS, they were piled up on the side of the block so that they could be counted dead or alive at evening roll call. I soon realized that this routine offered some good possibilities, and was sometimes able to lie down between the dead and the half-dead to get some rest.

The faces of the SS murderers and their helpers who armed with sticks beat us as if we were wild animals and have remained ingrained in my memory.

Unforgettable are the martyrs pale as ghosts from shock, dressed in striped uniforms, their heads and faces bloodied from blows. I remember them with broken glasses, missing teeth, the tall ones in short trousers, the small ones in clothing too large for them, holding in each hand a cap filled with pebbles so it would be easier to beat them. I search for words and comparisons with which to describe these murderous orgies; I am forced to think of starving wolves and lions as they tear apart the flesh of their prey.

One particularly dangerous form of torture was going to the toilet. It was a hole that measured about 10 by 20 meters and was partially covered by a roof. Wooden beams surrounded a round wooden ring, 10 centimeters across, which was fastened to the ground and on which the prisoners sat while relieving themselves. The chief of the toilet was an old, well-known, professional criminal called "Scheissmeister". He used a club to hit prisoners as he pleased, and he determined the type and length of our stay on the toilet. He was authorized to mete out punishments on the spot.

Other prominent criminals also came to the toilet to find alleged shirkers. As a first light punishment one was beaten on one's naked backside. The prisoners' only chance was to run away with their pants in their hands and join the others who were carrying sandstones in their caps. The other popular punishment was to hit the sitting prisoner in the face or chest so that he fell into the shit hole. During this ritual, laughing was permitted. As far as I know many of these people drowned and their bodies remained in the hole. In Majdanek even the toilet was transformed into a death trap.

Food was very poor, never enough and served irregularly with all possible trickery. We slept in three-plank-beds in three levels. We were not allowed to leave the blocks at night. As soon as the sun set, we were locked in. Wooden tubs were placed in the corners for human needs. The walls of these tubs were so high that it was impossible to relieve oneself standing or sitting. We therefore had to resort to all sorts of methods to reach the tubs. Dirtying the area around the tubs was punished by beatings. Nevertheless, it was always very dirty. The stench was horrible.

When the barracks were opened in the morning, carrying out the tubs and cleaning the block were the first reasons for beatings and torture. In comparison with the "Scheissmeister's" realm, however, the tubs were a bit better. It was part of the program at Majdanek not only to torture people while they were eating and working, but also to make using the toilet a terrible ordeal.

During the night one could hear the last cries of martyred prisoners and the shouting of the perpetrators. Even before sundown, wild screaming and scornful laughter were audible; these sounds came from the drinking parties of the eminent camp members. Suicides occurred again and again in the night. I will never forget Dr. Nick, a Jewish doctor from Warsaw, who was well known and respected for his helpfulness. One morning we found him hanging by his belt. On that day he had learned that his wife, with whom he had arrived at Majdanek, had been gassed.

The evening roll call was similar to the one in the morning, but in the evening, when the seemingly endless counting was over, several numbers were called. The prisoners who answered to those numbers had to run out and report to the SS camp administration. These officials announced the number of lashes and other punishments which they were to receive. For this purpose, there was a special wooden rack which the prisoner had to mount, constricted so that his legs and body were rendered immovable and his head hung down. Wania, a prominent Ukrainian prisoner in the service of the SS, sat on the head of the prisoner, while two SS men with leather whips administered 25, 50 or 100 lashes. The cries of these sufferers were loud and heartbreaking. The other prisoners were forced to watch and silently count the blows in unison while they listened to the cries of their fellow prisoners. One heard and felt every lash. The beaten prisoner was then taken, usually carried, to his block. This procedure was repeated 10 to 20 times each evening. Prisoners were also often hanged.

Every 10 to 14 days we were taken to have a bath. During the time we spent under the showers waiting for water, we were beaten. I do not know whether it was intentional or not, but the water always came out either ice-cold or extremely hot. After the showers, shirts were distributed. In early May, when it was still cold, we were given thin linen work shirts. As soon as it got warmer, we received winter shirts of blue and white canvas on the outside and warm flannel on the inside. The shirts had a double seam in the front, which was full of lice. We sweated, and were practically eaten alive by the insects. Because of bad food and having again caught typhus I had additional pains to bear: I suffered from scabies on my head, under my arms, on my backside and between my fingers. I got a can of sulfur ointment from a fellow sufferer. It burned like fire but brought some relief. Things were becoming intolerable. The lice were the worst part.

The Majdanek torture machinery was so well oiled that the SS spread terror among all prisoners of all nations in all of the five fields of the camp, even though there were not enough of them to carry out this intimidation day and night. They therefore chose so-called prominent prisoners in each field and each block who belonged to different nationalities. This privileged group comprised mostly the scum of mankind. They often acted in the service of the SS, or by their own volition, according to national prejudices. So it was that the Ukrainians took revenge on the Poles in Field 4 and the Poles on the Ukrainians in Field 3. Only Jews were not included in this international competition of hatred. We were beaten everywhere.

I will never forget the Russian prisoners of war, who in Field 4 were separated by an additional wire fence. I can still see them standing and clinging to that fence. They were emaciated, thirsting for water, yearning for food and dying like flies. Were those human beings, who created this inferno and observed this scene without emotion? Yes, they were the SS.

As a regular prisoner without any function or privilege, I hardly had any contact with the SS. Of course, I was cautious not to get too close so that I would not attract their attention. I never looked an SS man in the eye, not only out of disgust or aversion, but mostly out of fear. Fear was something we all experienced. I was lucky. Attracting the attention of the SS meant certain death. This is perhaps the most important reason I am alive today.

During the years in the ghetto and the camps, the cruelest experience was to suffer being hit by a fellow victim. There were of course prisoner-criminals of all nationalities. The most dangerous people who were conspicuous in their brutality were allowed to practice their sadism together with the SS. The first example of such torture that I observed involved the elder of our block, Moshe, called Poer, who was known for his crudity and brutality. He had been a porter in Warsaw and was a tall and fat drunkard with a sodden voice, a blue nose and rough manners. He addressed everyone as "son of a bitch" and deprived prisoners of bread and soup in order to provide himself with cigarettes and liquor. He hit us during roll calls using the excuse that we were not standing in a straight line. In reality, he wanted to become the pet of the kapos and the SS. I often saw Moshe Poer kicking Jewish prisoners in the face or stomach so hard they ended up half-dead; some actually died from their injuries. Naftali Gaslen, known as the "killer", was of the same caliber. He had been a thug in Warsaw. The two knew each other well. These brutal underworld types were especially at home in Majdanek.

One character, who was unique even in Majdanek, was a 15-year-old boy called "Bubi". He was small, fat, well dressed, and moved among the kapos, the prominent prisoners and even close to the SS. The 10,000 prisoners of Field 4 were under his command, sometimes for hours. They were forced to carry out all of his orders: "Attention! Caps on! Caps off! Right! Left! Keep in step! Double time, line march! March!" With club in hand and in a childish voice, he ridiculed and taunted us to the full satisfaction of the SS. We found out that this boy was a "pupil" (dependent and accommodating in every way) of the head kapo. He had earned his reputation with the SS by putting the nooses around the necks of his father and mother in Majdanek. As a reward, he became what he was. I do not dare to judge this macabre tragedy; perhaps a doctor or psychologist could. After the war I read a book by Paul Trepman in which he revealed that the head kapo and his protégé were later hanged in Majdanek.

Wania, the Ukrainian, was a murderer through and through and always shouted curses and insults used in the underworld. He had a hangman's face and a besotted voice. He would not walk three steps without beating or harassing someone within his reach. He would use his hands or his feet or would spit on prisoners, unless he had his thick wooden club with him, his preferred weapon. During the evening roll call, he was at his bestial best and in the right environment. His place was at the whipping table on which the prisoners were beaten. It seemed to have been invented for him. He would smile when the whipping started, because that was his opportunity to prove his importance, usefulness and indispensability. Cheerfully he would mount the head of the sentenced prisoner, moving like a winning rider on his horse. Above the cracking of the whip one could hear Wania's deep voice and, mingled with the victim's cries, his scornful laughter. Listening to this was enough to drive one insane.

I had never seen nor could I imagine a specimen such as Wania. Later on I read about similar persons in Solzhenitszn's *Gulag Archipelago*. But I too would come to personally experience Wania's brutality.

In the part of Majdanek in which I moved there were no paved streets, only sand and gravel. The only ones who drove were the SS; they had their bicycles, motorcycles, cars and trucks. The foot traffic consisted exclusively of marching prisoners and work details. Male and female prisoners were harnessed by ropes and wires to a wagon and used instead of horses. Wagons were filled with wooden barrels and crates containing excrement, liquid manure or other trash. Because of the heavy load, the wagon wheels sank deeply into the sand and the ropes cut into the flesh of the prisoners who, like horses, were driven on by the SS. It was an utterly depressing scene of inhumanity. The men and women prisoners on that street were a pathetic sight. Their heads were shaven; they were humiliated, sad and cramped figures in dirty, striped clothes, who had lost or been robbed of their human features and their dignity. These people were brought to Majdanek to be tortured until they ended up as smoke pouring out of the crematory's chimney.

Nowhere in the camp area did I see trees or grass, let alone flowers, fruit or vegetables. Nothing grew. I never saw any horses, cows, cats, chickens, geese, ducks, birds or bees. I neither saw nor read a written or printed word, nor did I experience a quiet minute or a secure second, not even while dreaming. Human life had no value. Since the victims were fenced in, the challenge of hunting them was lost; only the beasts' desire for fun, torture and killing remained. The camp was a playground for murderers – a reservation for death and extinction.

And the sky, was it ever blue? I did not know. I was ashamed to look; I could not stand the light. Blue was not our color, it was grey, and we inmates always looked down. We could expect nothing from above. Our future lay beneath us. The grey earth would soon consume our beaten bones or pulverized ash.

One day, gardeners were sought to form a gardening detail, for which I volunteered, although I did not have the slightest knowledge of gardening. I was accepted. The detail was to be sent outside the camp. I was happy to have been chosen and even considered the possibility of escaping, which the others probably did as well. The following morning the detail formed: we were a group of 50 people. Accompanied by two kapos and armed SS, we were let out of Field 4. Before leaving, we had to line up in rows of five and were counted repeatedly by kapos and others. We were then ordered to sing and march in step.

Marching in the open Dutch wooden shoes was torture. In order to avoid losing our shoes in the deep sand, we had to spread our toes wide and push them against the wood. After a while I thought that I would never be able to set my toes straight again. On the march we were repeatedly assaulted with rifle butts. We marched along the entrances to the three other fields, past the crematories and the adjoining warehouses, until we finally left the deep sand and reached a big field of ashes. The ground was warm and pliable. A strange smell hung in the air. We soon found out that a mass grave was located nearby. As special unit of French Jews, who were accommodated separately in the camp, was given the task of digging up the bodies, removing gold teeth and rings, and then burning the remains. These corpses were left from an earlier time, before Majdanek had crematories. The SS wanted to cover all traces of the mass graves and thus hide their crimes from the outside world. The French Jews who were chosen for the job were very strong, but they were liquidated and replaced a couple of weeks later.

Every morning we found the ground still warm and steaming. Depending on the wind direction and air pressure, the odor of burnt flesh became either stronger or weaker, but it never disappeared entirely. During these marches we also passed a part of the road which led from the arrival ramp to the camp. This was a street of Majdanek from which almost no one ever returned. We saw new transports arriving daily. We could even tell whether they came from the East or West. Those prisoners who came from the West wore hats, carried umbrellas and the women had fur coats; the trains from the East looked like prisoner transports from Siberia. There were also trains from the Warsaw ghetto where the rebellion was still raging. Occasionally we were able to call out a few words to the new prisoners.

All transports were guarded and accompanied by SS officials with their dogs. The poor prisoners walked silently amid shouted commands and the threats of loaded guns. But when we walked past them we heard quiet cries and questions of desperation. The impression we made on these people was clear. We felt sorry for them, because we knew what they could expect. One could find everything on this road to destiny: currency of all countries, valuables, dolls, purses, shoes, combs – everything that the new arrivals had lost or thrown away in desperation.

After a march of 5-6 kilometers inside the outer fence of the camp, we reached our place of work. It bordered the fence, was strictly guarded by the SS and was situated on the road to Lublin. It was not exactly a plant nursery. We were ordered to dig up the soil and build a flower bed close by.

Not far away from us, some Polish civilians were working with whom one could occasionally talk, if our kapos and foremen were bribed. Other work details could be seen in the distance. Sometimes even units of women walked past us. Despite the dangers involved, some civilians tried to establish contact with us to get jewels or other valuables in exchange for a piece of bread. Everyone assumed that these contacts could give him some advantage.

Using a spade while wearing wooden shoes was extremely difficult. Although it had become very hot, it was strictly prohibited to undress. We almost sweated to death in our flannel winter shirts, which were also full of lice. These ate their way into our bodies. It was a tragicomic battle against a plague that one could hardly see, but always felt. We called the lice the Nazis' allies, and indeed, that is what they were. It was a relief when we were allowed to go to the toilet, because then we could take off our shirts and get rid of some of the more aggressive lice.

Talk and conversation while working was not allowed; blows with wooden slats or spades, and cries of pain were their substitutes. After work we were forced to carry half-dead prisoners back to the camp, since they had to report at roll call, dead or alive. The following day they were replaced by new prisoners, since most of them had died in the meantime. In Majdanek there were no doctors, medicine or hospitals. Only a stone's throw away from our place of work we saw a peaceful road on which traffic passed and on which Polish farmers and their families went to church on Sundays. Fortune smiled on me in that I didn't have to dig ditches. Instead I was ordered to arrange flower beds. I defended myself as best as I could against the lice, blows, and hunger. The hardest fight was the one against starvation.

Next to Field 4 was a fenced-in barrack in which a group of specialists worked on hogs' bristles. This allegedly vital production had been transferred from the ghetto of Miedzyrzec to Majdanek. A former neighbor and good friend, Pesa Kaweblum, worked there. Thanks to good connections, I managed to get into that barrack for a short time. The employees there still had some gold and a few valuables, but little bread. Through my work as a gardener, I had become acquainted with a Polish civilian and a Slovakian Jewish prisoner who had a special function in the camp and suggested that I trade money and valuables for bread. Slovaks had been among the first builders of the Majdanek camp and those who still survived held important positions. Through my job as a gardener and my connections with the employees of the brush factory, I saw a chance to appease my hunger by trading. Thus, I decided to starve for a day in order to get a one-day ration of bread, which I then took to Pesa Kaweblum. In return I was given a gold coin. The next day I traded the coin to the Slovak in exchange for a four-day ration of bread. With two rations I was full, so I traded the rest of the bread and continued doing business in that way. That the bread was usually blue with mold did not bother me or my customers. We ate it anyway and at least assuaged our hunger temporarily.

One day, while passing a women's unit, I recognized a girl from my Hevra, Sarah Nissenbaum, who had been in Warsaw with me. When I first saw her, I was greatly surprised and unhappy to see a member of my Hevra in that hell, but then curiosity took over and I wanted to know what had become of the Hevra and my friends. They were the only people in whom I still had faith after my family was gone. I had taken these friends to my heart; all my wishes and dreams were linked with, and directed to, them. In the hours of depression, when I wanted to feel better, I would think about my Hevra. Then I believed that the Hevra might continue to make history and perhaps were still playing cat and mouse with the Nazis, maybe achieving some success. That I had had the misfortune to fall into this trap depressed me so much that I could only cry and pity myself. I sincerely hoped that my Hevra was safe from the fate that had befallen me.

In every arriving group of prisoners, I searched for familiar faces and I was happy when I did not recognize anyone. When I saw Sarah Nissenbaum, I thought that she must have felt the same way. They must all have assumed that I was dead, but there I was.

I decided to risk everything in order to talk to Sarah. I had to use this one unexpected chance to find out what had happened to the Hevra. I believed that I would then be able to die more easily or fight for my life with more faith. The uncertainty stifled me. When passing each other, we arranged a meeting close to where we were working and met on the next day. She spoke very fast, trying to use the minutes most effectively and to reduce the risk. She recounted the following story: The Gellermann brothers and Robale Elfenbaum, who had wanted to rescue me from Miedzyrzec, went to the Warsaw ghetto because of the hopelessness of the situation. After being denounced, Sarah also went to the Warsaw ghetto and from there was transferred to Majdanek by coincidence. My friend Mosche Ackereisen with whom I had lived in the Kidzinskis' house, returned to the suburbs of Radzyn in order to hide there. No one had heard from him again. The Kamienietzki sisters had given Aryan papers and their underground address in Warsaw to Miss Tisch of Miedzyrzec whom I had met in the ghetto. She was dark-haired and looked very Jewish. She was arrested on the train traveling to Warsaw and taken to the Gestapo in Miedzyrzec. Under torture she revealed everything. A few days later the Gestapo man Burger from Radzyn, who had helped both sisters and warned them not to procure Aryan papers, arrived at the Kamienietzkis' apartment instead of Miss Tisch. He arrested them and sent them to the Pawiak prison in Warsaw. In the end it was the same. All the Jews in Pawiak were killed.

That was my conversation with Sarah Nissenbaum. I gave her half a loaf of bread and then, with best wishes and tears in our eyes, we disappeared in opposite directions, regarding it a miracle that we had not been caught. Talking to a woman was a major offense for an inmate of Majdanek. In spite of all the good wishes I never saw her again. I had already expected bad news regarding my Hevra, but at least now I had some more details. That was the last information I received to this day. Even after the war I was not able to get any more news. Whenever a new book on Warsaw and the Holocaust appears, I look for the names of my Hevra. So far, I have found nothing. Retrospectively, I am satisfied that my Hevra, considering the circumstances, resisted and fought. This fact gave me the courage to persevere. I regarded it as my mission to continue fighting for life so that one day I could tell this sorrowful story.

In the meantime, I had a terrible fear of starving to death. In no case did I want to die of hunger. I smuggled valuables and the Slovak gave me bread which was brown on the outside and blue with mold on the inside. In Majdanek, it tasted like cake; I ate my fill and passed it on.

One day just after I had received a loaf of bread and buried it in a flower bed in order to smuggle it back to camp in the evening, an SS man who had been watching was suddenly standing in front of me. He took the bread and ordered, "Bend down!" Right there he gave me 25 blows with a black rubber hose which was 6-7 centimeters thick. Then he wrote down my number. I knew what awaited me that evening.

When we returned to the camp I was tense. I expected to receive a terrible punishment. Would I be able to withstand it? The evening roll call seemed to last an eternity; every minute was like an hour. As usual, numbers were called out and prisoners were whipped. Counting the lashes was bad enough, but being whipped... Finally they called my number, 1377. I ran to the front, took off my cap and, as was customary in Majdanek, stood to attention. The secretary, an SS man, held the notice in his hands. I was not asked for a comment, he just said, "50!" Immediately I was tied to Wania's torture table, with my feet in the raised block. He quickly grabbed my head and squeezed it between his legs. I heard my own cries of pain accompanied by Wania's laughter in rhythm with the blows of the whip. Thousands of prisoners counted: "One, two, three..." The pain was unbearable; I cried as loudly as I could. After 10-20 blows my cries were stilled and my pains were somehow different. I could not scream anymore; the blows seemed as if they were falling on a wooden board. I did not even notice when they stopped. I only knew it was over when Wania dismounted from my head. I saw the SS men wiping the sweat from their faces and rolling up their whips. They had beaten me with the thick part of the whip; the thin part was reserved for horses, the thick for Jews. Later in Auschwitz, I often saw one of these SS men. His name was Wieczorek.

I do not know how I got back to the rows of my block. Leo probably guided or carried me. With help from Leo, who was in the same block, I reached my plank bed. He also made it possible for me to stay in bed for a day. After 75 blows on my already frail body, my physical condition that day was pitiful. I felt as if my body was breaking into pieces; I could feel each individual part, nothing was whole and everything that I touched was bloody and injured. I was not mentally broken, however. When I came out of it, I saw people from my hometown, and my block gathered around me – Wolf Turkeltaub, Bunim Suessmann, Leibisch Baecker, Blumenfeld, and others. They asked me whether it would not be better to put up with the allocated rations than to risk such punishment. I told them that I thought that no way of dying was worse than starvation and that any means we could use to avoid that fate were justified. Given the possibility, I would continue doing the same. It is impossible to describe the ordeal of starvation. Only one who has experienced hunger can feel and understand it.

After three days, I returned to my work unit. I did not walk, I crawled. Because of the beatings, I could not sit down for the next 10 to 14 days. I did everything, literally everything, standing. My backside was black; the lashes could still be seen and counted. As paradoxical as it may sound, my wounds had a therapeutic effect, but I would not recommend this drastic remedy to anyone. My scabies, which mainly manifested itself as boils on my backside, had been pounded open by the blows. Although I had great difficulty tearing my shirt and pants away from the blood and pus which oozed from my wounds, no new boils formed.

From this "adventure" the elder of our block, Moshe Poer, inferred that I was an organizer. He did not know that I had smuggled moldy bread; he thought it was alcohol and sausage. He called me to him and said, "You son of a bitch, did you forget your block elder? If you want to live, you'd better remember him!" I did not forget him; the next day I disappeared from his block out of fear.

Pencils were rarely used in Majdanek. Hardly anyone wrote anything down, especially if it pertained to the treatment of Jews. No records were kept on that subject. In which blocks the victims were located and who was to die when were not important. Each one of us would have his turn. Thus, it was possible to disappear into another block in the same field.

During July and August of 1943 more and more prisoners were sporadically selected and transferred. Whether to the crematories or other concentration camps, no one knew. It is only natural for a prisoner to try to hide from his captors. But it was unimaginable that there could be a place in the world that was worse than Majdanek. With these thoughts I decided to neither appear for transport nor to hide. It did not take long before I was selected. This time my conscience did not torture me. After the war I learned that four to six weeks later, on October 16, 1943, all 18,000 Jews in Majdanek were shot in one day.

To this day I do not know how long I stayed in Majdanek. There were no calendars, we lived from one day to the next. It must have been three to four months, which was a remarkably long period of time for a simple prisoner in Majdanek. Sometimes I thought that I had spent my entire life there. That is how slowly and painfully time passed. But I was still living and it seemed that I would soon leave Majdanek alive.

The moment arrived. In a disorderly fashion we were sorted and loaded into cattle cars in groups of 40 to 60 people. We were treated like dangerous criminals. Four groups of prisoners sat in semicircles on the floor, holding their hands out in front of them so that every movement could be controlled. Talking was strictly forbidden. Two SS men with carbines sat on stools at the car door, watching us. Any improper or conspicuous movement was punished with blows of the carbine butts. It was actually a good sign that we were treated as criminals instead of an uncounted delivery to the crematory.

23 - Auschwitz

The next morning we arrived at Auschwitz. I knew a lot about that camp. When we passed the famous gate with the inscription "Arbeit macht frei" (Work sets you free), I remembered an old, childish illusion of mine which I had carried in my heart but was ashamed to share with anyone. I had wished to be in Auschwitz – to suffer, but survive – so that I would be respected as a Jew after the war, unlike others who disappeared or even cooperated with the Nazis. What a stupid, juvenile idea! For me, it was a sin then to be a Jew and not one of the sufferers. In my naiveté I went so far as to consider any Jew who did not suffer as an enemy and a collaborator. From this point of view and with Majdanek behind me, I pulled myself together with new hope. I wanted to live.

I do not know whether it was my will to survive or my fear of dying that was behind this new strength. My suffering had reached such a dimension that it seemed that a normal grave would not have been sufficient for me. All the plagues that Pharaoh visited on people I had experienced in my own body. Death could only be a relief. I regretted more and more that I had not understood that before. Was it worth giving up and ending my life after everything I had experienced? Was it not too late? Could there be anything worse ahead? I felt like someone who had missed the first and last trains – the train to death and the train to life. I had no alternative other than to push these thoughts aside as in the Hebrew adage, "What wisdom doesn't accomplish, time will!" I left my fate to chance.

We were gathered in a large, empty area where we were forced to undress and stand naked until the evening. It was very cold. There were two big wooden tubs filled with hot and cold water. One after another we were ordered to jump into both tubs. We received striped prisoners' clothes and canvas shoes with wooden soles. But we were not permitted to go further into the Auschwitz camp. We stood in a guarded area from which we could see the blocks and the prisoners.

We were then transferred by truck to the camp of Buna-Monowitz, about ten kilometers away. After the usual roll call with the endless numbers, a bath and delousing, we were examined for hidden objects. Again we impotently faced the men of the master race. In rows of five, every prisoner was carefully observed and examined as if we were chattel at a slave market. Those who were accepted had a number tattooed on their left arm. My number was 128262. Some emaciated prisoners, the so-called "Muselmänner", were chosen, taken away and never seen again.

At the naked parade in and after the bath, my marked backside attracted special attention. I was taken around by prisoners with special functions, exhibited to other prisoners and pitied. I thought that it could not be as bad there as in the ghetto of Miedzyrzec and in Majdanek.

The 400 to 500 prisoners from the Majdanek transport were accommodated in one large tent. We were in quarantine and were separated from all other prisoners. Our whole group was taken to the morning roll call and then to work, about 4 kilometers away. We had to labor in a deep, muddy canal, knee-deep in water. Our wooden shoes kept getting stuck in the mud. As soon as we pulled out one shoe, the other one sank and we slipped repeatedly. Under these conditions, we first had to fill cars with clay and then pull them upwards. Because of the steep slope there was always a danger that the heavy cars would roll backwards. There were many injuries. The SS were stationed on dry land on either side of the canal and watched us. They continually called up prisoners, worked them over with wooden boards or rifle butts and threw them back into the canal. The kapos stood down below, cursing the prisoners and beating them again. It was hell. In the evenings we had to carry beaten, wounded and half-dead prisoners on our backs so that they could be counted at roll call. For those injured prisoners, that roll call was almost always their last.

Our strength declined rapidly; many prisoners were pulled out of their rows and never seen again, taken directly to the crematory in Auschwitz. The rows of prisoners from Majdanek were noticeably thinned out. I also felt as if all my strength had gone. Extremely hard labor under the eyes of the SS officials, insufficient food, no communication with fellow sufferers – all this and more that I cannot even begin to describe could not be endured by any human being for longer than one or two months.

After about six weeks, the quarantine was over. Our camp and work detail were dissolved. According to our profession, we were divided into other details and transferred to different blocks.

The Buna-Monowitz camp, which we just called Buna, contained 10,000 prisoners who were leased as slave laborers to IG Farben Works by the Reichssicherheitshauptamt (The Main Security Office of the Reich). The objective was that we should first work ourselves almost to death to the advantage of IG Farben and then be liquidated. I was put in the Elektro-Kommando 128. Our kapo was Erich Kohlhagen, a Jewish dentist from Halle. We were about 50 prisoners. After the daily roll call which, as in all other concentration camps, lasted for hours in the rain and cold, we marched approximately four to five kilometers to work, to the accompaniment of music that was played at the entrance gate. Five to ten prisoners at a time were assigned to a civilian master whose orders were to be followed absolutely. Our commando detail was under the command of Obermeister Killian, a feared man who normally only spoke to the kapo.

For a certain period of time, my group was under the command of Master Hoppe from Leipzig. Hoppe's conversations with us were limited to the allocation of work. He never inquired about our living conditions; he knew enough about them and did not need to ask. He came one, twice or even three times a day, stayed for about 10 to 20 minutes, then disappeared. He always showed up in a blue jacket, usually wearing high boots. In one hand he held a yardstick, in the other a spoon and fork riveted together. Hence, he could eat with either implement, but never with both. Was this the eating culture of the new European society planned by the Nazis? I met one of these masters who preferred to say three words too few rather than one word too many and who saw much more than he wanted to in Leipzig after the war. He was working as a conductor on a streetcar. I greeted him and told him who I was, since I always considered him harmless. At the next stop he disappeared, and another driver took his place. All these masters had been ordered to be deaf and blind. The majority obeyed this order. They had ears that were unable to hear, eyes that could see nothing, and tongues that could not speak.

Another master, with whom I was able to exchange a few words, came from Gleiwitz and allegedly used his position to avoid being drafted. He had an assistant, a Ukrainian girl, who had been deported as a civilian. She – her name was Maria – was very open with me. Often she offered me a part of her scanty bread ration, which I almost always refused. We talked about war and politics and encouraged each other. Only once, shortly before Christmas 1944, when the winds of fate had changed and the war was going against the Germans, the master from Gleiwitz gave me a piece of cake. It was the first time in years that I had tasted cake.

I regard it as imperative to make special mention of one Master Kuss from Leipzig. He was small, slim and well known for his friendliness toward us. Whenever the SS came near us, he always cried "Six". "Six" was our code word for approaching SS. Although I never accepted assistance from him, I knew that he had helped some of us. One day he disappeared and we never saw him again. Rumors that he had been shot persisted. It was impossible to get more details, but it was well known that he was an anti-Nazi and that he had helped our people. We were sad to have lost him. He was one person whose continuing goodness could have restored our faith in mankind.

I was fortunate to work in a hall, protected from rain and the cold, which might be one of the main reasons I survived. Those of my fellow sufferers who were forced to work outside laying cables, unloading cement, coal, iron and so on hardly had a chance to survive. Given the circumstances and the lack of nutrition, no one could last more than three or four months.

In the winter it was even worse. Although it was strictly prohibited, we tied paper from cement sacks to our chests and backs for protection against the cold. People died by the score, and those who survived looked like mere shadows of their former selves.

Some prisoners were so emaciated that their bones were visible and their feet resembled matchsticks. Others had bloated stomachs, swollen legs and furuncles. Diarrhea was rampant. Smokers who exchanged their small food rations for tobacco and enthusiastic dealers who bargained with their basic rations contributed to their own destruction and involuntarily delivered themselves to the Nazis.

It was impossible to live on the normal food rations and trading was even worse. It was self-torture for those who tried to divide their rations into small pieces and eat them at intervals. During the day they carried their tiny morsels with them and at night they hid them under their heads to keep them for later. They never allowed themselves to be distracted and were unable to sleep at night. This self-imposed contest between stomach and soul became an additional nail in their own coffins.

A missing pair of glasses, a lack of medicine, too much rumination, some apathy, traces of weakness and defeatism, losing control over oneself just once, branded a person as a Muselmann and that was the beginning of the end. Our executioners attacked us like beasts. Our chances of surviving were about the same as those of an inexperienced tightrope walker, trying to cross an ocean on a rope.

But thinking back to Majdanek and the quarantine period, I could almost be content despite everything. In order not to attract attention I always restrained myself and kept my distance from the kapo. He was very strict, but he tried to be fair. Nothing that happened around him was of any importance to him, or at least he pretended that it was so. He was not able to help anyway. With his work detail, he was like an adamant father who establishes a certain order. His attention was concentrated on making sure that all his prisoners were clean, well-dressed, well accommodated on the block and that we completed our work to the satisfaction of the master. His main insistence, however, was warning us not to be conspicuous in a negative way. He was feared, but at the same time appreciated and respected by us. I remember that he did everything humanly possible to spare his work detail during the selections. When he addressed me on my first days at work, my voice quivered – I do not know whether it was out of fear or respect – and I made the mistake of addressing him as "Herr Kapo" ("Mr. Kapo"). With the words "What kind of a Herr am I for you?" he slapped my face twice so hard that I almost fell down. I understood immediately that these two slaps were the first justified blows I had received in a concentration camp. My camp education had failed me. Those two slaps, which I both understood and forgave, were truly warranted. There is an unwritten law in prisons and concentration camps that says that in these places there are no "Herren". I simply was not aware of the etiquette of Auschwitz and had violated that law.

Herschl Bergasin, a very fine man who looked compulsively clean, was one of the leading workers and the kapo's first helper. He survived and today lives in Montevideo. Thousands of civilians, foreign workers of all nationalities, British prisoners of war and Russian Vlasov soldiers worked at the Buna plant. Our food rations were really starvation ones: in the morning a piece of bread with a little margarine and a bowl of soup at night. Our IG Farben employer was so generous that he also contributed a small amount of soup for lunch, the so-called "Buna soup". It was grey in color and contained no potatoes or other edible additions, not to mention vegetables, fat or meat. It was said it was made from spinach, probably because of its color. The technicians, engineers and directors who came to the plant wanted to neither eat nor taste the soup. That was fortunate for them, because it was almost pure poison from IG Farben.

Through our work, contact with the civilians around us was unavoidable. Again I began risking everything in order to avoid dying from starvation, as I had promised myself not to do. I smuggled shirts, blankets and sweaters out of the camp and traded them for bread and margarine. As soon as I was satisfied and still had a reserve for the next day, I stopped smuggling. I kept this promise and made it the guiding principle of my life in the camps.

Organizing food was, of course, very dangerous and severely punished. If one was caught, it meant a brutal beating or transfer to a penal detail or a detention camp. One always gambled with one's own life. Unlike in Majdanek, I was fortunate enough never to be caught in Buna. My contacts sometimes brought me only bread or margarine. Thus, it also happened that I would eat an entire pound-package of margarine only.

Through our contacts, we often received news of the war, which filled us with courage and new hope. We even were able to obtain newspapers like the Völkischer Beobachter and the Oberschlesische Zeitung through civilians and smuggled them into the camp.

We felt great satisfaction when the plant was bombed several times. We prisoners did not hide, but enjoyed seeing the SS disappear. It would have been easy to escape during those air raids, but where to? There were no Jews left with whom one could hide. Our world had been destroyed long before. For us, the bombings marked the beginning of the end of our suffering about which, despite everything, we never stopped dreaming.

It is perhaps difficult to understand why we were happy about the bombings, since we also could have been their victims. The bombs, however, hit people regardless of race, belief or nationality. Bombs have no delivery address, they hit everyone. All other torture, beatings, deportations, gas chambers and shots targeted exclusively Jews. All people with my past have learned about and are prepared to bear the sufferings attendant upon life, provided they are also given the opportunity to enjoy its pleasures. To suffer with people regardless of station or race did not hurt that much.

One day in 1944 a barrack was built and fenced in with barbed wire in the middle of the camp at Buna, close to the formation field. About twenty women, supposedly of all nationalities, were brought in and a brothel was set up. Prominent prisoners, elders of blocks and kapos from different countries were allowed to visit them with coupons obtained from the camp administration, but the mixing of races was prohibited. All races were represented among the women except Jews. Jews were not allowed to satisfy their sexual desires. Such feelings were supposed to be suppressed by the bromine that was added to their soup. But it helped us to joke and be of good cheer. Long live the Jewish humor, it is healthy to laugh.

Our first job in the Buna plant was to install provisional electric lighting in buildings 702-703. As we entered the cellars, we were in total darkness. Floors had not yet been installed; small and large concrete blocks and many holes proved obstacles for us. Before the first light had been installed, several prisoners had suffered broken bones. We never saw those people again.

Together with several other prisoners I was later given the task of setting electric motors on concrete bases. It was labor which could not be easily evaluated. We sabotaged the work as much as we could, talked during working hours, made plans and even dreamed about the future. The main subject in regard to the past, the present and the future remained food. Everyone told each other how well and how much he used to eat. According to what was said, hardly anyone had ever eaten dark bread or inexpensive food like potatoes. The greatest wish for the future was to eat a whole loaf of white bread, preferably with butter, whenever we wanted. We would salivate as we spoke. This is how hungry people talk.

Our plans for the future mainly concerned Israel; we wanted to have a country of our own, to never again have to depend on the mercy of others. We envied all those who were already there. It was a dream which hardly anyone believed would come true, although no one doubted the end of the Nazis. Some dreamed of traveling throughout the world as survivors and reporting on the almost unimaginable events and massacres in the ghettos and concentration camps. The following generations had to be told of the greatest genocide of all time. The conversation almost always ended in a mood of depression, especially when we talked about murdered family members, our horrible present, and what we would have to face if we survived. The biggest optimist in our group proved to be a Pole who always repeated: "Fellow sufferers, don't worry. Whoever has talent in his fingers will never fail in life!" He was supposedly a professional pickpocket.

Even in the hours of desperation, with death awaiting them, some Jews in the towns and ghettos put on their tallises and with a prayer book in their hand and the "Shmah Israel" ("Hear, O Israel") on their lips, they went to meet their end. Others were so upset by their own suffering and family tragedies that they rebelled against God and lost their faith.

In Kommando No. 128 there were some Jews – mostly from Hungary and Greece – who figured out the date of Yom Kippur, commemorated it and fasted. They did the same on Tisha-b'av, marking the day the Temple was destroyed. They even wanted to observe Passover by not eating bread. On those days, one could read the words of prayers on their lips. Kapo Kohlhagen showed respectful understanding in that regard. These people demonstrated an uncompromising dedication to the faith and an iron will by imposing additional fasting on themselves. Holding the bread ration of Auschwitz in one's hand and not eating it was an extraordinary exhibition of heroism.

In one group from my detail I worked with the French Jew, Spiro. He claimed that he had lived in Paris and had led the communist youth movement there. He was known among us as a pleasant and educated man with whom one could discuss any topic for hours. He criticized me and all the others who smuggled shirts, sweaters etc. out of the camp to exchange them for bread. His criticism was most acute when someone was caught smuggling and was punished accordingly. Unfortunately, that happened quite often and the punishments were severe. Spiro believed that smuggling was immoral, since every stolen piece of clothing meant a prisoner for whom that piece was lacking. He was actually the only one who held that opinion, which was based on a general idea of concentration camp justice. It was easy for him to castigate since he found considerable support for his beliefs among his friends, the French doctors in the medical building. Almost every evening after roll call, he went to his friends and reported to us the next morning about the political situation and whatever else he had learned. He said that he belonged to a French resistance group that had been formed in the medical building. He comforted us with good news and predictions about the end of the war. I do not know whether he survived.

Although a great deal has been written about Auschwitz and the adjoining camps, the morning and evening roll calls must be described again and again. During the long, cold and always dark hours of the roll call we leaned back to back on each other to bear the bitter cold a little bit better, or we stood very close together, spreading warmth with our breath. Even that was prohibited.

It also happened that a prisoner would escape. We were then forced to stand in formation until he was caught, and until the alert for the whole area was called off. It was not unusual to stand for three, six or even eight hours. The same ritual took place when prisoners were hanged. Hangings in Buna were always carried out during the roll call. Everyone had to watch. I shall never forget the time when three young Jews from Berlin and Cracow, Diamant, Grossfield and Fleishman, were about to be hanged. The first cried out: "Comrades, heads up, we are the last ones!"

The German Kutschera, the elder of the camp, a professional criminal with a green patch on his chest, enjoyed putting the rope around a sentenced man's neck after an SS official had read the judgment. "In the name of the Reich's leader of the SS, prisoner number … is sentenced to death by hanging." For some unknown reason, one day Kutschera wanted to give some prisoners the honor of placing the rope around the three condemned men's necks. But no one wanted to perform the dirty deed. We stood in rows of five in the roll call area. As soon as Kutschera approached the front rows, all in the other lines stepped back. The same happened when he tried it in another place. Each step toward the crowd made the entire group step back. This happened spontaneously, and was a kind of passive resistance. Kutschera found himself in an embarrassing predicament and was finally compelled to go to the scaffold himself. Under the eyes of the prisoners and the three sentenced men, he put the ropes around their necks.

Unforgettable is the old inmate Chaim Wideslewski, the block chief. He was a decent character always ready to help, acting as a go-between with the camp's elders. One day there was an alert; Chaim along with two Jewish and two Polish inmates from the upper stratum of the camp had escaped. After an Appell (assembly) that lasted for many hours we were finally dismissed. A few days later we saw the two Poles. It was rumored that they had been recaptured in Cracow quite drunk. Only later did we learn what had happened:

the two Poles had murdered the two Jews, their fellow inmates, in the forest, most probably to rob them. The Poles were hanged in the camp.

At another time a 16-year-old boy from Hungary who had not been at camp for too long was missing at the roll call. We had to stand in the rain and cold for hours. Finally it was discovered that the boy was a "pupil" of his kapo, who wore the green patch of a criminal. He had raped, killed and buried the boy in the sand. The SS dogs found him. The kapo was stoned publicly and beaten to death. This too was SS justice.

With the war dragging on, the situation in the camp worsened. Selections increased, especially in the mornings and evenings while marching out or in. The blocks were searched for weak, emaciated prisoners, the Muselmänner. They were ordered to undress, and their clothes were taken from them. In the rain and cold, they were driven naked onto the waiting trucks and transferred to the crematory in the main camp at Auschwitz. The victims and everyone in the camp knew exactly where this journey would end. Heartbreaking scenes took place. Fathers, brothers, relatives and friends saw each other for the last time.

Every European nation was represented at Auschwitz. Some prisoners received occasional food parcels. These non-Jews were fortunate; their chances for survival were much better than ours. Jews got nothing but beatings. We had never heard of the Red Cross, let alone received anything from them.

Many new transports arrived, especially from Hungary. Some of the prisoners who had been there for a long time ran against the electrified fence of the camp in desperation and perished there. If they were noticed by the guards, they were shot and left hanging on the fence. Generally there were only hours, perhaps minutes, for one to pull oneself out of despondency. The long days and nights, weeks and months passed in complete apathy, desperation, pain and preoccupation with the hopelessness of our situation – it was a vegetative state without end. In such a state of mind there were times when the final penalty, death, became insignificant and no longer mattered; on the other hand the petty abuse became more painful and upset us to a greater extent.

One of these cruel pranks was the order to sew shut all the pockets in our clothes, since it was forbidden to have them. Our only possessions were: undershirt, underpants, the jacket and trousers we wore, a striped cap, a soup plate and a spoon. Famished, emaciated and freezing, our two pants pockets were the only place we could use to warm our hands when we were not working, standing to attention or removing our caps in front of SS officials.

One day I noticed several boils on my neck. When they got larger and looked more dangerous, I went to the medical building. The prison doctor told me that the boils were a consequence of poor and insufficient food, and also of typhus. He could not give me any medication or better rations. Thus I would probably be selected for the gas chamber unless the boils were operated on, i.e., cut open. I agreed, even though anesthesia was not available, and the bandages used were made of paper. I lay down on my stomach on a cot. My hands and feet were tied to the side bars and my head was held tightly. With unbearable pain, the boils were lanced.

For weeks and months thereafter, I was afraid my paper bandages would be discovered. It would have been sufficient reason for selection and that area of the neck was watched intently when we marched past the camp gate. I lowered my head and pressed the bandages down while pulling my collar up. I was fortunate and managed to get through. When I received my first identification card after the war, those scars were registered as distinguishing marks. I just laughed. Today I still bear the marks on my neck.

In Block 11, where my work commando was accommodated, the camp's band was also housed. The musicians, 30 to 50 people from all countries, always played when the prisoners marched in or out. There I got to know a Pole, Buson from Bromberg, with whom I soon became friendly, but not without a definite reason. The band members were considered half-prominent and were spared from working in the plant; they always remained in the camp. My friend Buson provided me with underwear, sweaters and scarves in exchange for which I usually gave him tobacco.

The elder of the block, a Jew named Glueckstein, had converted to Christianity before the war, but the Nuremberg laws made him Jewish again. He was a clever man of small stature and strikingly meticulous, who knew how to climb upward. In the camp he was known as "Pipel". He obviously sympathized with the camp prominents, the big providers, corrupt SS officials, kapos, elders of the blocks and other functionaries, all of whom managed to eat, drink and live well in the camp.

One Sunday, Kutschera surprised us with a visit to our block. The green patch on his jacket showed that he was German and a professional criminal. Pipel jumped up and shouted, according to the regulations, "Attention! Caps off!" Kutschera walked slowly together with Pipel between the plank beds and inspected everything very carefully. For some unknown reason, Pipel directed Kutschera's attention to me. The elder of the camp looked at me and discovered I was wearing a sweater, which was prohibited. This fat, brutal giant with hands like bear's paws used to execute his own brand of justice on the spot. He slapped me in his special way. He always slapped the right side of the face so hard that the victim fell to the left. In the next moment he slapped the left side of the face so that the beaten man fell backwards. His victims were not allowed to fall down. They had to endure his blows while standing so that he could see and enjoy the fear in their eyes. Like a soccer player who kicks with the right foot as well as the left, Kutschera could hit with his right hand as well as his left. He did so from both sides in a fraction of a second. After several slaps he allowed himself a break of satisfaction, laughed and emitted sounds that reminded one of a wild and angry animal. I do not know how many slaps I got.

When I was sitting on my bed recovering, Pipel came to me and excused himself for having directed Kutschera's attention to me. He regretted that I had to be the victim this time. I had been in the camp long enough to know that the camp elder never walked into a block without having some score to settle. Pipel was right, someone had to be chosen. It was my misfortune to be standing in the wrong place.

Even among professional criminals, people who were as brutal as Kutschera were not to be found in unlimited supply. I cannot imagine that he ever thought of a possible end to Auschwitz. I do not know what happened to him, whether he disappeared together with the SS or entered another criminal underworld.

Pipel's gesture impressed me; I simply was not used to having someone apologize for beatings. Apparently it was his clever way of not making unnecessary enemies. However, I never knew how I should classify him as a human being. He certainly did not belong to the 36 Righteous Men of the Bible, or at the court of the Rabbi of Gur. Pipel allegedly survived the war and crawled away to some place where nobody knew him. I think he knows why. Whether he was an opportunist or a swindler, he had style and belonged to the elite.

Like Pipel, the elder of the room, Kogut, was also from Lodz. His world revolved around his hometown and he divided fellow sufferers into two categories: those from Lodz and the others. He was a decent, simple Jew who loved order and tried to preserve his good reputation. If he helped someone, he could only have come from Lodz. Lodz was always with him. If he lowered the ladle deeper into the soup pot, it was only because the recipient was from Lodz.

In those times, when the turnover of people was fast due to selections and deportations, friendships usually only lasted a short while. There were some, however, which endured longer. At that time I befriended Jakob Hendeles, who later became my brother-in-law.

With the arrival of each new transport we hoped that we might meet a relative or a friend, since that was the only way we could hear some news about the world outside the camp. But we rarely learned anything, since most of the new arrivals came from other concentration camps. We longed to see friends again and were disappointed when we did not, but we were never sure whether it was really a reason for joy or concern. Where could our friends be? Were they rescued? Did they escape or die? Were they deported, beaten to death or were they existing, half-dead and starving in some concentration camp? A newcomer was lucky if he was assigned to a good Arbeitskommando. That could be decisive for his future. It also happened that a new prisoner was recognized as having had an infamous past, and as having served our persecutors by tormenting us. For such prisoners, the bell had already tolled. The score would be settled with them.

I always looked for compatriots and silently hoped to meet a member of my Hevra. Unfortunately, I waited in vain. Then one day I met some friends from Radzyn: Abraham Schuhmacher, Getzel, and Jesaja S. Rosenkranz. Since I was by now a relatively experienced prisoner, I tried to support my newly-arrived friends in word and deed, and to help them with a piece of bread and bit of soup every now and then. One day before roll call these friends introduced me to Ajzyk Kupiec. He was an active Zionist, and had left Radzyn in the early thirties and emigrated to a kibbutz in Palestine. For special reasons and under unusual circumstances, he had left Israel and participated in the Spanish Civil War. In the meantime, he had become an enthusiastic communist. Together with Spanish veterans, he found asylum in France and had lived in Paris where he was arrested by the Gestapo and sent to Auschwitz. He remembered my older sister Idessa; we knew each other's families. Even earlier he had been known to us as a sensation. That morning he told me that he had come from the camp of Jaworzno, a subsidiary of Auschwitz where the prisoners worked in the coal mines. I never saw him in Buna again; reportedly he was transferred to another camp. After the war I heard that he had survived. This made me very happy.

The year 1944 was close to ending when the war took an unfavorable turn for the Nazis. We felt that the worst was behind us, and this strengthened our resolve to persevere and survive.

24 - Leaving Auschwitz

In January of 1945 the bomb raids became more frequent, and we heard the artillery fire come closer. Each day brought new rumors about the camp. Unrest and tension grew. We said to ourselves, "Don't take any risks, or attract attention, just try to hang on. Maybe we'll make it after all, even though it seems impossible."

Many of the German masters had gone missing in the plant where we worked; they were supposedly drafted. Discipline, as well as production, declined. In the plant one saw uniformed men who were members of the anti-aircraft division. The civilian non-Jewish workers encouraged us. The Russian front was drawing closer. The normally strict German order of things crumbled. The camp files were packed or burned. Selections were reduced. Apathy spread among the military as well as the civilian masters of the plant. The camp was supposed to be evacuated. All the sick people who could walk were discharged from the medical building; seriously ill patients were shot. Some people talked about evacuation by train, other about liquidation. Things developed differently, however. The situation did not allow for a systematic evacuation, since there were no longer any means of transportation available. Marching on foot was the only possibility. It was probably also too late for liquidation.

On the morning of January 16, 1945, after a short roll call, we started marching in rows of five. We noticed that the SS could no longer keep up their customary standards of planning and execution. Ten thousand famished prisoners with ragged clothing were turned over to the icy cold. We marched west. Our SS guards accompanied us in cars, on motorcycles, on bicycles and in horse-drawn wagons, shooting those who were too weak to continue and thus delayed the march. These people were pulled out of the rows and shot on the side of the road or in a ditch. Their numbers were not small.

Those who had sweaters or blankets were of course better prepared to withstand the cold. Those wearing wooden shoes suffered the most. Marching in them, kilometer after kilometer, was worse than torture. Many prisoners limped or fell down or slipped on the icy roads. It was a dreadful and desolate sight: thousands of emaciated prisoners with their heads shaved and in tattered, striped suits slowly marching westward.

After a march of about 40 kilometers, we reached Nikolajew where we spent the night in a brick factory. We had only a roof over our heads; we therefore huddled close together in order to warm each other with our bodies. In our exhaustion, we were happy just to lay our heads down somewhere. The only thing we had to eat was the double food ration we had received before leaving camp. We hardly saw any civilians on the road; it was probably closed to traffic because of us. Along the way we noticed other groups of marching prisoners from Auschwitz and its auxiliary camps.

The sound of artillery fire grew fainter. The next day we walked another 30 kilometers and reached Gleiwitz. All weak, limping and complaining prisoners were shot. Discipline had to be maintained. It was an infinitely strenuous march in the cold, snow and ice. For many it became a death march, for the rest it was torture.

Gleiwitz was a border station between Germany and Poland and the gathering point for prisoners of all the concentration camps, including the men and women from Auschwitz and its satellite camps. Although we had not seen any transports of women, we were told that they would also be arriving.

In Gleiwitz the confusion was great upon our arrival. Among the thousands of prisoners one saw many SS men, but no civilians. At one place bread was available, at another one could get blankets and shoes and at still another, soup and tea. We saw SS men who were carrying provisions: two big loaves of bread and two cans filled with either lard or meat. Some prisoners jumped on this food; a few officials fought them off, others put up with it. No punishment followed and no one was shot contrary to the usual custom.

We were in a big camp with minimal fences outside of town. Earlier, foreign civilian workers had been lodged in these wretched barracks. The camp was not big enough to accommodate all the prisoners, so those who found a place to lie down were happy. From minute to minute our fate became more insecure. Gleiwitz in such confusion could never be our goal. Perhaps the SS no longer had control of the situation. The most likely possibility was that we would be shipped to another concentration camp. There were, however, no trains to be seen. Everyone speculated about a forthcoming liquidation by poisoning or shooting. Naturally we thought about Majdanek, where 18,000 Jewish prisoners were shot in one day.

We kept hearing artillery fire. Some of us desperately hunted for a hiding place, but hideouts were few and far between. In the chaos one could not form a group or meet with friends to discuss plans. Eventually I found a spot in the attic above the bathroom of an old barrack. When I climbed up, I met two friends from the camp who had provided themselves with bread and wanted to stay there until the Russians marched in, unless, of course, they were discovered first. Who knew what was right? These two comrades – Pruzycki and his cousin – persuaded me not to stay with them. Even though they would not admit it, the main reason they rejected me was that I had no food reserves so my hunger would surely be a burden to them. That was the first time that my camp know-how had been proven wrong. In the camp, I lived by the rule of eating everything as soon as I got it. I would stuff myself with food, instead of saving the small portions and fighting an even bigger battle with myself. At least I can say that no one ever stole my bread. Here in Gleiwitz with the Pruzyckis, this practice became a liability. The Pruzyckis and two other prisoners survived. Two days later they were liberated by the Russians. I met them by chance after the war and of course forgave them for their seemingly selfish behavior.

Rather than become a burden, I left the hiding place. I reflected on the situation: "In this chaos, I could go to the city, but with my clothes, shaven head, physical condition and appearance, I would be recognized immediately as a prisoner and, consequently, would either be arrested or shot." Only someone with friends in that town or region on whose support he could depend had a chance to flee. I continued to look for a hiding place, but without success.

After two days in Gleiwitz, the SS had regrouped, the trains arrived and we were treated more severely: the slackened reins were tightened once more. Prisoners in groups from their former camps were collected and loaded onto the trains. After 19 months in Auschwitz I left Gleiwitz – traveling toward uncertainty. I had the impression the destination was unknown even to our masters.

On January 21 or 22, 1945, on a bitter cold day, we were packed like sardines into open train cars, 150 to 200 people in one car! There was no possibility of sitting, let alone lying down. Our only protection against the rain, snow and cold were tattered blankets which we held over our heads. The only heat was body heat. Before the start of our journey we received some food. Gleiwitz, a camp used for food storage, would soon fall into the hands of the Russians. Our train was guarded by SS men who sat outside the cars in little guardhouses. We headed west. After the first few days, hunger tortured us but we suffered mostly from thirst. From continuous standing and immobility, our legs became numb and swollen, our blood stopped circulating. Basic human needs caused problems, but in the open cars they could be relieved with relative ease. In this situation, friction and aggression became more prevalent. Powerlessness, apathy, melancholy and hysteria afflicted us all. Some cursed, some shouted, others scratched their neighbor's faces. Many died standing.

Sometimes hours passed before we realized that the quiet person standing beside us was dead. The bodies were laid on the floor and the living stood on top of them. Thus we could soon move our arms more freely. Occasionally the train stopped for several hours, but usually on the outskirts of towns and villages, so that we saw little or nothing of the civilian population and vice versa. From our zigzag course we could tell that we were traveling without direction.

Our situation was indescribable. Half-dead people from concentration camps fought for their lives with their last bit of strength. Packed in cars with dead bodies at our sides and underfoot, we were exposed to hunger, thirst and cold. I cannot remember that I received anything to eat on that trip; perhaps I got some water or soup. I cannot really recall. We simply could not think straight anymore. I know for certain, however, that SS officials guarded the train at every stop. Only a few prisoners jumped off or disappeared when we stopped and they usually did so only to end their lives. Most felt paralyzed and could not find the strength to jump.

A decisive factor for survival was the place in which a prisoner stood in the car. In the center, one had the advantage of heat, but next to the car walls there was more elbow room. The latter places were especially coveted. Prisoners standing at the walls were the first to receive food. Since there was never enough of anything to go around, only those who had a little more luck or freedom of movement received something. People lost control. Everyone went nearly mad or worse. All of us fought against the numbness and for a little water, bread and indeed life.

This horrible, seemingly endless journey took us first to Vienna, then to Czechoslovakia (Prague and Pilsen, as far as I can remember) and from there to Hamburg-Neuengamme. We were turned away at every camp because of overcrowding. For hours our train remained on the sidetracks, then we continued to travel from south to north, and from north to west with neither direction nor knowledge of our destination. Although we were told to cover ourselves with blankets when passing cities, people often saw us and our cries for bread and water could not be ignored. I can remember only one incident, in Czechoslovakia, where slices of bread were thrown from a bridge into our cars. Otherwise we saw only silent, almost petrified faces staring at us. We must have been visible, since our train was very long and moved slowly, being driven by two locomotives, one in the front and one in the rear.

The duration of the trip meant that the number of people jumping off the train increased. These people had suffered enough, they wanted to be shot.

To assuage our hunger and thirst we ate the snow which covered the rusty car walls. We lapped up the orange liquid. This possibility was restricted to those standing along the walls. We stood there motionless, like wooden statues. Where would we find the power to survive? With the thought of jumping in my mind, I half fell asleep and saw my sister Sonja with another girl whom I like very much. Both of them implored me, "Hold on, stay where you are! You still have to suffer a bit. It will take some time, but you will make it!"

I woke up and did not know whether my dream had lasted three minutes or three hours. I awoke a new man with new hope and with the goal not to succumb, but to continue fighting. This dream was a source of hope and determination from which I drew strength until the final liberation; it helped me a great deal. I also reassured myself with the old motto that had helped me in Majdanek: it is not only a question of life. Each death of a Jew gives Hitler and the Nazis exactly what they want. I wanted to survive at least for that reason, to spite our enemies out of "daffke". I also did not want the Nazis to decide the manner in which I was to die. The journey continued, as did my struggle to survive.

After many concentration camps had rejected us and after eleven days of suffering, we finally landed in Nordhausen (Harz) at Camp Dora. Out of the 10,000 prisoners who were loaded on the train in Gleiwitz, purportedly only 6,000 survived the journey. The enormity of the tragedy became clear only when the cars were unloaded. We then realized how many dead bodies were standing at our sides or lying under our feet. The dead were piled up and removed by a special work detail.

We who were still alive felt half-dead when we left the cars. Hardly anyone could walk, we could not feel our limbs; every part of our bodies was wooden. Our legs refused to carry our bodies. We were so apathetic that we did not react to anything and allowed everything to be done to us. We did not care, but our tormentors did.

25 - Camp Dora / Nordhausen

After the usual concentration camp ritual – bathing, searching, delousing, receiving a number, being counted again and again – we were lodged in barracks of 200 each. The camp was located at the foot of a mountain and still more concentration camps were close by. This camp of 4,000 to 5,000 prisoners did not have a crematory or a gas chamber. We were supposed to work ourselves to death there for "Führer und Reich" in accordance with the Endlösung.

I was aghast at the appearance of my fellow sufferers there: their heads had a line shaved into them that was known as a lice street. Until then I had seen only shaven heads, but here I saw crisscrossing shaven lines lending a sense of the ridiculous to these poor people.

The factory was located three kilometers from the camp in a mountain and consisted of a kilometer-long underground work street. In the middle of the mine was an assembly line of tracks. At approximately every 200 meters, islands for machine shops, depots, etc. had been constructed. The plant manufactured V1 and V2 missiles or projectiles. In the beginning I worked on the production of the V1, which looked like a miniature metal airplane. I was soon assigned to the V2 and worked on a big island at the main entrance to the factory.

The prisoners comprised all nationalities. There were no foreign civilian workers in the plant. The foremen were exclusively German civilians. Our presence and our work were well suited to the secrecy of the plant. Since we were already condemned to death, we could only take what we saw to our graves. Our deaths were part of the plan of operations. We felt like people who were going to die soon, but still had duties to perform.

Innumerable SS men watched our every step. Every stage of production was inspected by the SS; they even worked themselves.

For the first time, I saw SS men using screwdrivers and measuring instruments. About six meters above the assembly line were inspection stations from which passing V2s were inspected and measured with cables. From there, the SS could oversee every work station and all phases of production.

It was strictly prohibited to talk with civilians. Conversation among prisoners, except when it referred specifically to the work, was also not allowed. During my entire stay at Dora, I never spoke a word to a civilian. My job was to screw down the numerous covers on the V2 with an automatic screwdriver. I was the last worker on the assembly line. After a final inspection, the missile or projectile was loaded onto a double car, camouflaged with a net and then transferred to Peenemünde. Only the basket of dynamite at the front of the bomb was missing. With the basket in place, the V2 looked like an egg. In the beginning, 20 to 30 bombs a day were produced; a few weeks later the number increased to 60-80.

Soon we saw that many of the bombs were coming back. We would scratch a mark on each bomb with our screwdrivers to see if the same ones were indeed being returned. Our assumption proved to be right. We were never given any reason, but it gave us a certain satisfaction.

The group in which I was working was supervised by a strong, anti-Semitic Latvian foreman. Okrongly, a somewhat older hairdresser from Lodz whom I knew from Auschwitz, worked with me on the assembly line. Since he could not keep pace with the work because of his age and weakness, he was often harassed and beaten by the foreman. While trying to defend him, I also received some heavy blows from the Latvian. I finally worked so fast that I had time left to help my colleague. He survived Camp Dora, but not Bergen-Belsen.

After the morning roll call, we received a small ration of bread before marching out to work. The next meal, soup, was scheduled after the evening roll call. That meal was rarely served, however. The secret factory had been discovered by the Allies. Almost every evening, while we lined up for our return to camp, an air raid kept us from leaving the factory. The plant itself was safe from bombs, since it was underground in a mountain. But we were not allowed to leave it. Instead of granting us some rest during these raids, the SS took us back to work immediately. The raids lasted until midnight and it was 1 or 2 a.m. before we returned to camp. By then we were happy just to lay our exhausted bodies down for two or three hours. At about 4 or 5 a.m. we were woken up for the morning roll call, in order to be back at work by seven o'clock. We thus worked 16 to 18 hours a day, all week long. We started in darkness and finished in darkness, without seeing the sun or daylight and without breathing fresh air.

After a certain period of continuing air raids, the soup and bread were distributed in the morning. The SS amused themselves by giving us one loaf of bread to be distributed among five or six prisoners, instead of our usual rations. We were to divide the loaves ourselves. Anyone who has suffered from hunger can imagine how that worked out. During the distribution of bread, heated arguments arose, which certainly pleased the SS. The first and only function for which I volunteered in camp was the distribution of bread rations, which I must say I carried out to the complete satisfaction of my group. My friend Rafael Olewski took over the same duties in his group. I am sure that if the rations had been placed in a troy scale, no difference in weight between the portions would have been detected. The bread was cut exactly, and divided and distributed by drawing straws. I always took what seemed to be the smallest portion and thus earned the trust of my group.

I saw how hungry and nervous people literally got into each other's hair and lost all control. When hunger prevails, normal rules of human behavior no longer apply. Looking at it now, I probably relinquished only a few grams of bread, but that was enough to reestablish an esprit de corps in our group. It was a very small act, but a gratifying one.

The regime in this plant and camp was very strict. The head of the camp was a brutal SS man whom we called "Horse Head". His head looked like a cross between a horse's head and a donkey's. Unfortunately, I cannot remember his name. He was omnipresent and struck us brutally.

On Sunday, when the plant was closed, we were given the honor of carrying the bomb sections and fiberglass into the plant in preparation for the following week. The casing of the V2 was elliptical and consisted of two parts, the top and the bottom sections, which were about two meters in diameter and twenty meters long. The aluminum surface of the bomb was painted a light green. The sections had very sharp edges and lay camouflaged in front of the factory in a big field. A mountain of fiberglass insulation was also stored there. Several motors of different sizes, connected by cables, were built into the V2 bombs, which were then filled with fiberglass insulation.

The brutal chief of the camp with the horse-like head personally supervised our work. Each section was carried by sixteen men, eight on each side. On such days, the tall prisoners regretted their height. Shorter prisoners could at least duck so that they would not bear the brunt of the weight. The number of blows meted out, however, was the same for everyone. Because of his height, my friend Jakob Hendeles had a particularly difficult time. The heavy bomb sections cut deeply into his shoulders. There were no aids for carrying the sections and, in any case, using any was prohibited. According to "Horse Head", we "lazy pig Jews" could not, and did not, want to work and, because we "as Russian communists and American capitalists" were responsible for the war, he was willing to teach us how to work. After carrying the bomb sections, another "honor" was bestowed upon us. We were forced to carry large rolls of fiberglass into the plant, running while we did so. The rolls cut into every part of our bodies; the small glass splinters were especially dangerous to our faces and eyes. A small piece of fiberglass in the eye could torture a person for weeks and it was impossible to remove. These Sunday marches were the private amusement of "Horse Head". Sundays were harder to bear than the normal 16-hour working days.

In that camp of silence, "sabotage" was always in the air. Without being asked or told anything, prisoners of various nationalities were hanged, supposedly because of sabotage, but actually as a warning. In order to frighten us, the victims were left hanging for a full day so that they could be seen by everyone.

One day I experienced one of these executions right on the island where I was working. The spot was probably chosen because it was located at the main entrance to the tunnel, through which all prisoners had to pass. A band had been requested for the occasion. A scaffold was erected against the wall. In the early afternoon, many SS officers arrived. Among them I suddenly recognized the Gestapo chief from Radzyn, Fischer from Erfurt. In 1942 I engraved his name in my memory after seeing Lichtenstein, the elder of the Jews, prepare a package of gold and jewelry for him; now in 1945, I had come across him once again. At occasions of this kind, characters are not easily forgotten. We were released from our positions for a short time. When we returned after almost an hour, 22 people of all nationalities were hanging in the air, only five to eight meters from my work station. Deadly silence prevailed until the assembly line started moving and the usual noises were heard again. It was atrocious working next to that macabre sight. The dead bodies of 22 men dangled and twisted in front of our eyes. No words were uttered. We all watched but remained silent.

Without any contact with the outside world, we learned hardly anything about the war, but a few things had started to change. According to our calculations, about 60% to 70% of the marked missiles were returned. The faces of the SS men and the German civilians showed neither enthusiasm nor joy. Suddenly electric motors and other parts were missing and the missiles remained stationary on the assembly line. Soon we had to stop working, since we had run short of everything. We had suffered under the Germans and their quest for perfection for so long that we welcomed the chaos that ensued.

26 - Bergen-Belsen

So that we should not fall into the hands of the Allies, we were to be liquidated or evacuated. Soon the moment arrived; again we were gathered in the roll call area and quickly loaded onto waiting train cars. This time the trip did not last long. After a day's journey, we arrived at Bergen-Belsen. This concentration camp was hopelessly overcrowded and we were not accepted. The right hand no longer knew what the left hand was doing, so we were sent to an adjoining Wehrmacht compound. As the soldiers of the Wehrmacht marched out, we moved in. The confusion was unbelievable; this time it was disorder with German perfection. We were moved into clean barracks, equipped for human beings with excellent bathrooms and clean beds stacked three on top of each other. After all we had experienced in the preceding year, this was sheer luxury. There was no mention of the usual camp rituals, no roll calls and no work, but also no food. The kitchen and food supply were guarded by the SS and Hungarian soldiers, Hitler's allies.

Hungry people searched every trash can and rubbish heap for potato peels or anything edible. After two or three days, there was absolutely nothing left to eat in the refuse of the huge compound. Most of the time we just lay in our beds, listening to and enjoying the approaching artillery fire. We lived on the good and bad news, with reports changing from one hour to the next. But the hunger remained constant. One rarely saw the SS anymore; we were guarded solely by Hungarian soldiers. Every now and then in the confusion soup was supposedly distributed. Perhaps one person heard about it, a second saw it and a third actually received it. Perhaps. When it came to camp hierarchy and maintenance, some of the prominent prisoners tried to take over. Among them were many Poles, so-called "functionary prisoners". It was surprising to find that they were in such good condition. The other prisoners, especially the Jews, were so weak and exhausted that they could hardly stand. Still there was nothing to eat, because there was absolutely nothing anywhere.

My friends and I were emaciated – our average weight must have been about 40 to 50 kilos. We spent most of our time lying in our Wehrmacht beds. We decided to wait, be passive and not to take any risks. The following four or five days passed without any food. Hunger and the headaches it caused became more unbearable with each passing hour. I suddenly fell into a deep depression and developed an indescribable fear. I believed that if I did not eat anything that day, I would not be alive on the next one. With the will to survive, I decided to act immediately. I dragged myself to the kitchen building which was guarded by prisoners, mainly Poles. The outer ring around the building was composed of Hungarian soldiers. It was impossible to enter the kitchen through the main entrance. On the other side of the building, however, I noticed some small cellar windows that were open. Turnips were supposedly stored in that cellar. Those were the only edible things in the camp that I had seen. They seemed to be my last hope for survival.

From time to time prisoners crept through a window into the cellar. Afterward they came out the same way or through the entrance with turnips. Some of the prisoners left beaten, others not. That I had to know someone in that building in order to come out in one piece was something I tried to forget. Besides, I had noticed that my Polish camp associate, "Buson of Bromberg" as he always introduced himself, was in the building. Perhaps I counted on him at that moment. I did not reflect for very long. I gathered my pants tightly at the bottom to make room for the turnips. Thinking of Buson, I jumped into the cellar. I had managed to get in, but how would I get out? I put a few turnips in my pants and started to negotiate with the Poles and Ukrainians who were waiting for me with clubs in their hands. Would they beat me to death? How many blows could I still stand? It was my misfortune that only one or two other people were in the cellar with me. Previous observations had convinced me that if three or four people climbed out of the cellar together, it was possible to escape with only a few bruises. Unfortunately, I was not that lucky. Then my friend Buson suddenly appeared in front of me. As I looked at him confidently, a shower of blows rained down on me. I was bounced from one cellar post to the other with blood streaming down my face. I thought that I was unconscious for a short time, but Buson's vulgar Polish tirades against the Jews rang in my ears. I did not see him leave. That was the Pole, Buson of Bromberg.

When I was able to move again I considered the situation. It would have been stupid to leave the cellar empty-handed after that beating. Again I filled my pants with turnips and told the guards in front of the windows that I would give them all the turnips if they would let me come out without hitting me. They agreed. First I stuck my head out, then half my body, while throwing the turnips farther and farther in front of me. The guards collected the turnips while holding their clubs. With the last and largest one in my hand, I ran out of the cellar, after being pummeled by Buson. One blow more or less was not that significant anymore. I considered the operation successful.

One single turnip was the spoils of my victory. I returned to my barrack, lay down on my bed, enjoyed my reward and felt like a hungry animal after a predatory raid. I became more confident with each minute that passed and felt that finally I had made it. With this one turnip I could survive for at least four days. On the third day the first British outposts marched into Bergen-Belsen.

It was April 15, 1945, and I was alive.

27 - Free

When I think back on the pain and torture in the ghetto, the suffering in Majdanek, the fear in Auschwitz, the hunger in Camp Dora and in Bergen-Belsen, it seemed that on that day in April the world started over again for me and my people. The joy was overwhelming, there were only laughing and crying faces. One would have to be made out of stone not to be impressed by those faces even in our awful surroundings. I added up the sad balance: I had lost my whole family: father, mother, grandmother, brother, two sisters, brother-in-law and niece. The way in which all those relatives were torn from me might have been unique, even in that inferno. My dear Hevra, all twelve friends, had been brutally killed by the Nazi murderers, either individually or in a group as martyrs, along with hundreds of relatives, friends and acquaintances.

On this day the whole world changed. It was if a volcano had ceased to spew out its lava, sirens had ceased to blare, and a million people had stopped to mourn. Suddenly there was quiet and calm.

That I am still alive can only be attributed to coincidence and fate. In none of the often precarious situations in which I found myself did I do anything heroic. Everything I did was a result either of "EIN BREIRA" (hopelessness) or "DAFFKE" (an act of defiance).

It was a great consolation and satisfaction to me that my friends and I resisted the Nazi murderers with all the available, albeit modest, means. That my Hevra was not able to experience the day of our liberation filled me with sorrow. I can only thank a fortunate fate for allowing me to live to see it. There were two things that bolstered my self-confidence and for which I was indebted to good fortune: firstly, that I never served the Nazis intentionally or voluntarily; secondly, that I never acted against my people and my fellow sufferers.

I had never been a member, assistant or employee of a Judenrat or the Jewish police, nor had I been a kapo or a block or room elder. That was the source of my moral strength. Never, during those hard times, did I forget from where I came, who I was and where I belonged. I was always on the side that had it rough but whose cause was just. Even if I had been able to choose, I would have felt better as one of the persecuted than as a persecutor or an accomplice.

As a survivor, perhaps I also made some mistakes and even caused some injustices to occur, but my intentions were always good. I fought and resisted with all my limited means. I know that there are many others who experienced similar or possibly even worse hardship; I respect and admire all those who engaged in greater resistance against the Nazi butchers.

The day of our liberation was one of heshbon-hanefesh for all survivors. At the end of that terrible time we became aware of how easy it was to show kindness in a normal and free society, though we realized how difficult such behavior had been in the hell of the ghettos and concentration camps. The diabolical and ingenious extermination apparatus of the SS was created to replace the humane with the inhuman and the good with the bad.

Everyone wanted to survive. Many tried at all costs to live better and seem more reputable than the others. Many failed because of their modesty and some struggled with themselves to the limit of their consciences. It was a hard lesson for everyone and every character was unmasked facing such an ordeal. Those who survived the test earned a degree in being human.

I could be satisfied with the grade of my own heshbon-hanefesh. Whether I owe it to my upbringing or my modesty does not have to be asked. For remaining alive, I am indebted to coincidence. In any case, I regarded my own survival as a victory in an otherwise costly war.

Like a stranded man among the stranded, like a sufferer bound to all sufferers, I stood alone in front of the shambles of my life which had stopped when I was seventeen years old and from which nothing could be salvaged or repaired.

My own Holocaust had started almost five years before. I was very young then, but in the meantime had aged much more than those five years. The time of youth, when the basis for a human being is created and his personality is formed, the time of cheerful memories, of school, of first love – this period of laughter and pranks from which everyone derives pleasure for a lifetime – this period did not exist for me and my contemporaries. It was taken from us because we were born Jews. We spent this period in a hell among devils in human form. Those years were dead years.

No nightmare, no horror story, no fantasy can be compared to life in that inferno. Those five years seemed like a lifetime to me; I thought that I had been born and always lived there. Sometimes I would strain my memory to remember the time before 1939.

Then, my world was comprised only of Jews and non-Jews. I saw the world divided into the persecuted and the persecutors, the tortured and the torturers: on the one side, the beaten and the dead, on the other, the sadists and murderers. We Jews were always given the role of the persecuted. Even after the liberation I did not dare to think of changing roles, although I had wished it before: just once I wanted to play the other part and then die. The outrageous injustices committed against us hurt us more than all the resulting suffering. I could forgive neither God nor mankind for what I had witnessed and experienced during the extermination of our people. There is a lot of injustice in the world, but for that kind there is no consolation. Like a wounded animal I thought that I had to show my wounds to the world with its morals, political parties, organizations and religions so that not only the crimes of the murderers, but also the injustices committed against us Jews would be recognized.

To wake up from this trauma, conscious of the necessity to see and judge the world and people differently, to overcome the past was my problem and that of all my fellow sufferers.

Lonely and forgotten by the world, we stood there as liberated newborns and as objects of interest, enduring everything with indifference. Our liberators, the assigned helpers and social workers of different organizations were very good to us. They surrounded us as if they were bystanders who had unintentionally caused an accident and then tried to save the injured.

The destiny of Jewish survivors differed completely from that of other nationalities. The rescued people of some countries and nations were transported back to their homes with music and pomp. We Jews were the only ones who had neither home nor family; we did not want to return to our cemeteries and we did cling to what remained of our Jewish identity. This was facilitated by the representatives of Jewish organizations and the Jewish Brigade from Israel.

Attempts by non-Jews after the Nazis' fall to inspire us with pleasant-sounding slogans about the equality of all human beings regardless of race, color and religion were ineffective and rejected out of hand. We did not care to hear that anymore. The bitter experience of recent history had proved that our 2,000-year-old concerns and problems were and are different from those of others and that these differences cannot be reconciled. Ours remain specific. We are not to blame for this.

After those terrible years of suffering, we Jewish survivors and newborns wanted to live consistently as Jews; the large majority of us wanted to belong to the Jewish community and to live our lives as Jews. Under no circumstances were we willing to wait and to rely on the so-called "common sense of man", which we felt hardly existed nor included us. Jewish existence should never again depend on the alleged "common sense of man".

Auschwitz survivors did not need nor did we want to wait for the "Aharit Hayamim" (the Last Days), as the Bible calls them. The role of the eternally weak, pitied and innocent people which we were forced to play never did us any good in the past or in the present. We came to Auschwitz as a weak people. During and after Auschwitz we realized that this role had to be changed.

Only after liberation did we become fully aware of the tragedy in Bergen-Belsen. I was very fortunate to be lodged in the Wehrmacht compound instead of the concentration camp proper. About 50,000 prisoners were gathered at Bergen-Belsen; they lived in intolerable conditions. Every second inmates died within six weeks of their liberation, after they received food, medicine and care. The English did their best, but they were neither able to cope with that inferno nor had they been prepared for it.

With a great deal of satisfaction we saw that the SS men, our persecutors of yesterday, were forced to bury the dead bodies in mass graves. Only the former "functionary" inmates were physically able to even consider revenge. That desire among most prisoners – who, like me, weighed about 40 to 50 kilos – was dissipated in the presence of light, the sweet soup that the English gave us to accustom our empty stomachs to meals, normal digestion and functions, and the desire to be human again.

About three or four weeks passed before I could leave the camp for the first time. Close by, I stopped in front of a house. With a slight yearning for revenge, but also with fear, I opened the door and found the house almost entirely empty. Next to the front door I found a woolen cap that I exchanged for my striped one. I looked for something to eat, but found nothing. In front of the house, however, I saw a cage containing two rabbits. Were I not a Jew, I would probably have slaughtered the rabbits and taken the meat with me. I had seen a lot of blood in the previous few years, but killing animals was impossible for me. I took an empty sack, slowly opened the cage and managed to get the two rabbits into it alive. It must have been either my persuasive words or the will to commit a first act of reparation for a Jew that made them jump in.

I carried the sack on my back. The rabbits jumped in all directions and were so lively that I almost fell. Nonetheless, I succeeded in getting my booty back to camp. There were about ten people in the room when I arrived. All of us were hungry, but no one was able to kill the little animals. We opened the sack and set them free.

In the days after the liberation, when we realized that there was no Jewish home and family without causalities and hardly any with survivors, friendships between us developed naturally. Everyone sought to lean on someone and we all felt lonely. Thus, my friendship with Jakob Hendeles became stronger. Despite the differences in our personalities and views, we moved together into our new lives; we were both tired of the camp and wanted to leave. But in 1945, shortly after the war, existence on the outside was not easy either. Obtaining food and clothing was a big problem. I remember that I went to a cookie factory in Hanover and asked if I could buy some. Of course, nothing was sold at that time. However, I was given a pound–box of cookies at the gate. They were a delicacy. I then sent Jakob, and he too received a box. That was a big prize. One hour later we changed jackets and caps and it worked for a third time. We tried once more, but by then the game was up. Again, we were able to laugh.

I recall how we once got hold of a bicycle on which we rode together to Celle and back. Celle, which was about 20 kilometers away, was the nearest city of any considerable size. From there we often returned with half-filled sacks of turnip peelings from which we brewed our own schnapps. We had learned about this process from a

Russian, for a price, of course. The first batch we made was 100% poison. What came after that was basically dirty water that we then mixed and, according to our Slavic customers, tasted excellent. In any case, it was better than the eau de cologne that they sometimes drank, even if our brew did not smell as good. We sold our schnapps. Our Polish clients made fun of us "stupid Jews". Here we had vodka and instead of drinking it ourselves we were selling it. The Poles thought that we had learned nothing from the war: we had been stupid and we were still stupid.

Our short-lived production presented us with a big advantage. Even without drinking the concoction, we constantly suffered from headaches and were always drunk from inhaling the vapors. On the days following production, we had additional fun getting drunk just by drinking plain water. Anyway, through our brewing talents we soon came into possession of a motorcycle, which caused a great sensation and made a lot of noise.

The original concentration camp at Bergen-Belsen had been evacuated in the meantime; all inmates, except those who were in nearby hospitals, were transferred to our Wehrmacht compound. A Jewish administrative committee was organized under the leadership of Josef Rosensaft. Although we had rented a room in Celle, we spent most of our time in the camp. There were also women who had been brought there from other camps. Sometimes it happened that prisoners and SS members with long lists of crimes were discovered. A prisoner who recognized his former tormentor settled his account in his own way on the spot. The same was true for prisoners with outstanding debts. The SS men were fortunate, however, that their methods of punishment could no longer be used. They were lucky that the new democratic, humane laws were applied to them. We were the last ones to suffer from their murderous tactics. The SS people were surprised, since they knew what they had done, and expected the sort of punishment they deserved.

One day I read in a newspaper that witnesses were being sought to testify again the SS official Fischer. I volunteered immediately and shortly thereafter was called to Dachau as a witness. I spent ten days there and was questioned by Allied officers on several occasions. I testified to everything I knew about Fischer in Radzyn and Miedzyrzec and, of course, I related what I had witnessed in Camp Dora. I told them everything I knew about him. Since I realized that a confrontation was bound to occur, I suffered many sleepless nights. I still lived in the past and would now have to face the principal murderer of my family and compatriots. On the other hand, I wanted to know what had happened to those special Jews or Sonderjuden to whom he had promised his protection. What happened, for example, to Simon and Andzia who were married before being imprisoned? At the time of the investigation, I already knew that no one who relied on him had survived. I wanted to talk to this creature (I refuse to call him a human being) and spit in his face. I even considered dirtying my hands and hitting him in the face.

The day finally came. Accompanied by several officers and guards, I was led into a room in which about 60 SS and other war criminals were lined up in two rows. Some were wearing uniforms, others were in civilian clothes, but all had shaved heads. As instructed, I started at one corner, took my time and looked each one straight in the eye for as long as I could. It was actually the first time I had peered so closely into their eyes. I always considered that the main reason for my survival was that I rarely came into the direct view of an SS official. I was simply overlooked. Those who had come to their attention were all killed.

I walked slowly from one to the other, looking for the one murderer among the many. I had almost finished one row when I began to doubt whether I would recognize him. Could I tolerate listening to one word of his about Jews who were beaten to death under his command? Suddenly I recognized the last one in the row – it was Fischer. I needed all my strength to point him out, but I did not question him, nor did I spit in his face as I had planned. I saw him for one fleeting second through a fog and then I blacked out. I awoke on a couch in an adjoining room. Later I learned that Fischer was eventually extradited to Poland as an SS criminal. Mayer Turkeltaub, a cousin of mine, testified against Fischer at the trial.

When I returned to Bergen-Belsen after my testimony, I felt a great sense of relief. The following weeks and months remain in my memory not only as a period overshadowed by a sad past, but also as one absolutely free of worries and concerns about the future. As if recovering from a serious disease, we lived in convalescence with free housing in the Bergen-Belsen compound and received free food from the Joint Distribution Committee in America. Slowly we returned to human culture. We remembered music, theater and books. The opposite sexes attracted each other again; sexual life was revived and soon marriages took place in abundance.

My friend Jakob and I alternated between living in the city of Celle and Bergen-Belsen. We befriended two sisters, Dora and Balla, and spent a great deal of time with them. Dora was usually at Jakob's side, and Balla at mine. Our friendships flourished. At that time I could not imagine marrying a woman who had not shared my experience. I was therefore grateful that Balla had traveled the same roads as I had, including the journey from Auschwitz, and shared the same experience of liberation on that day in Bergen-Belsen. We were married in 1946 in Marburg. My friend Jakob became my brother-in-law when he married Dora.

After the liberation of Bergen-Belsen, when we went for walks there, we were often stopped by former prisoners who thanked and kissed Balla for the help she had given them in the camp, risking her own life in the process. During a bus trip to Hanover, a woman recognized Balla, threw her arms around her and thanked her for saving her life. That was a very proud and moving moment for me. We experienced a similar incident in New York some years later.

My wife has often told me that she is indebted to her sister Dora for saving her life. My children and I are eternally grateful to her.

At that time we lived in a classless society. We all possessed the same – nothing – ate the same food, wore the same clothes and experienced the same concerns, joys and goals. Socially and in all other areas equality, comradeship, helpfulness and harmony prevailed. It was life on equal terms – a community that had died was resuscitated. This time of transition was soon superseded by a new and brighter period.

As if by the signal of a starting gun, the race for money and for what one could do with it had started. Again, everyone wanted to amass more wealth and achieve more than his friends and neighbors. Was that a sign of a return to normality? I do not know. In any case, Bergen-Belsen soon became a base for a flourishing black market. The incentive for this change came from Jews arriving from Russia for whom this type of business was an integral part of their very struggle for survival.

If we had been transferred to Israel before or during this period, we could have served ourselves and Israel well. Although we were skeptical and suspicious, we were consistent, willing to adapt and ready for a new beginning.

28 - The Trip to Poland

I never felt any desire to return to Radzyn. I felt even less attracted to the Polish country, its culture and its people. My experiences during the war had strengthened my conviction that Poland was no place for me or any other Jew. In spite of all this, I allowed Jakob to talk me into a trip to Poland. His family had hidden valuables in his hometown of Warthegau (Zawiercie) and he wanted to reclaim them. Two of Balla's brothers were also said to have survived there. So I decided to accompany Jakob.

I donned my best clothes: a British uniform and shoes which were three sizes too big. We had received these from the English. It must have been about September 1945. We traveled mostly by train through Czechoslovakia to Poland. The trains were neglected, often without compartment doors and popular with Russian soldiers. One also saw many dubious characters among the passengers, who would let off steam in their own particular way. I remember one scene in particular: several Russian soldiers enjoying themselves with a couple of girls in a compartment without a door. Each of the soldiers took his turn covering the doorway with his coat. At night the lights often went out and luggage would disappear. It was a trip full of adventure. Everywhere we went, we explained that we were traveling to Poland for a family reunion. We repeated this story on the return trip, and Balla's brothers were part of it.

After arriving in Warthegau, we were able to retrieve part of the valuables in a somewhat audacious way, which was not without risk. We soon realized that the Poles who were living in the formerly Jewish apartments regarded them and everything in them as their own, legally acquired property. Fights would occur when returning Jews tried to reclaim their belongings. Such disputes were usually settled brutally, often ending in murder and always in favor of the Poles. For them, the best Jews were the ones who did not return.

The few Jews left in Warthegau could be counted on one hand. They lived apart and were ever fearful, especially when they tried to claim their former possessions. As we heard, the situation was the same in all Polish cities. The Poles asserted that hundreds or even thousands of Jews had returned, when it was actually only a few. In their blind hatred of Jews, they saw each Jew as a hundred or a thousand. The organized Polish resistance was really more directed against the Jews than the Russians. Whenever they stopped busses or trains, they looked for Jews first. I was prepared for almost anything, but the rampant anti-Semitism, especially after all that had happened, surprised even me. I could not imagine that it was going to be that bad.

With a heavy heart I decided to travel to Radzyn. Perhaps by some miracle some members of my family were still alive. I knew their fate, but maybe there was someone left from the Hevra, a relative or a friend. Finding out was reason enough for me to make the trip. The only people I wanted to see were the few decent Poles who had helped us, assuming they were still alive. Perhaps I also wanted to take one last look at the town of my childhood and thus end a sad chapter in my life.

My journey to Radzyn passed in a state of fear, but without incident. During the long trip, I remembered that I had been on that same train twice before, both times as an Aryan and fearful of my life. Now I traveled as a free man but again I was afraid. The reason was the same as before: I was born a Jew. In the past the Nazis had stopped the trains, sorted out the Jews and killed them; now it was the Polish resistance group, Armia Krajowa (A.K.). This thought filled me with hatred for those people and for that country.

Having reached my parents' apartment, I did not have a peaceful minute. All my memories came back to me. The whole tragedy of our family, the news of arrests and deaths, the bitter tears, the worries, the suffering and the pain were alive again in my mind. No, I could not stay there.

After not a moment of sleep, I went into the town the next morning and could hardly see a friendly face. Aside from the Jews, almost all of the original inhabitants were still there and they surely did not miss us. Those who had taken over the Jewish shops showed no enthusiasm, even though they had always dreamed of owning these stores and superseding the Jews in the economy of the town. Despite the boycotts, they were not able to compete with us; even then, they did not seem to be prospering.

Standing in front of the office of the power plant and seeing the steps on which little Sarah had waited for me every day, and remembering how she had held out her thin arms to me, passing the houses of the Gestapo and the house in which my brother had hidden, thinking of my Hevra and entering my parents' home, I found it hard to breathe. I felt as if I was in a cemetery and each house was a monument. I could never live nor laugh there.

On the street I met a Pole who had known my father fairly well. He worked in a liquor factory and was wearing one of my father's coats. When I cautiously drew his attention to that fact, without intending to reclaim the coat, he became suspicious and pretended not to know me or remember my father. Finally, he insulted me using the usual, spiteful Polish vocabulary.

A special experience was my visit with the technical manager of the power plant, Mr. Domaratzki. I knew from the past that he was a vehement anti-Semite, even though he had been employed by Jews. I secretly hoped that his anti-Semitism had been tempered during the war, but that, unfortunately, was not the case. He seemed very surprised to see me alive. In my curiosity, I imposed myself upon him by asking questions about Lichtenstein and the imprisoned Jews (Lichtenstein had been the co-owner of the power plant and

Domaratzki was an employee). Domaratzki had known all these people and must have known all about them, but he repeatedly avoided the subject. Instead, he kept referring to the Polish girl photographer from Warsaw who had helped us and purportedly was arrested for that reason, after her brother, my companion in Miedzyrzec, had been caught. That is what Domaratzki implied, but did not want to discuss. To my question as to whether the girl was still alive, and if so, where she lived, he reacted in a suspect way and said that I would find out soon enough.

I wondered whether he really knew anything. I felt very uneasy about the question and answer game we were playing and became wary. His words sounded superficial and cloyingly sweet as he tried to convince me that he was glad to see me. In reality, my reappearance did not please him at all. It was obvious to him that I would not stay in Radzyn for any length of time, but he wanted to know exactly how long. Everything seemed to depend on that, perhaps even my life. With all my powers of persuasion, I convinced him that I would stay for at least ten days.

I could tell from his face that he was planning my end. He could achieve it within ten days, perhaps even sooner. At that moment I had the same instinct that had saved my life before. I could imagine what was going on in his anti-Semitic mind. My intuition convinced me of his evil intentions. He believed that he had ten days to carry out his plan; I knew, however, that I would have to leave town the next morning.

When I returned to my parents' apartment, I found a few Jews who had returned and were staying there temporarily. The news I heard from them was hair-raising. They told me that a new, strictly anti-Semitic organization had been founded. Domaratzki, with whom I had just spoken, was, of course, a member. Under the guise of a resistance group fighting the Russians, this organization had as its primary goal the liquidation of all Jews returning from hiding or concentration camps. Two Jewish families from Radzyn, the Ponczaks and the Kleinbaums, who had survived by hiding on a farm, were the most recent victims of this new anti-Semitic organization. Together with all their relatives, the two families had been shot by the A.K. After my conversation with Damaratzki, I had no doubt that I was next on their list.

By accident, I heard that a Russian truck was leaving for Warsaw at five o'clock the next morning and that paying passengers were being accepted. I inquired about the place of departure and sneaked there in time. About twenty people were in the truck, most of them women who, with their baskets full of food, were going to the big city to trade their wares. Silently I stood in the corner. I did not want to speak to anyone, nor did I wish to be spoken to. The two Russian drivers were drunk as usual. Trying to pass another truck, we hit a telegraph pole. One woman died immediately, and many others were thrown from the truck and injured. I was alright, but was disgusted with the drivers. I made my way to the next railroad station and traveled by train to Kattowitz, and from there to Warthegau.

I had, and still have, feelings of gratitude, friendship, love and recognition for the very small group of Poles who proved their humanity and compassion toward their tortured, Jewish fellow men.

I also think about the Poles who helped my friends and me when we were in grave danger. Although their number is smaller than in other countries, a good number of Poles did risk their lives to save Jews. Today one often hears how rescued Jews pay back their Polish saviors who are now experiencing difficult times. In Israel, some of these almost saintly helpers were immortalized by Yad Vashem on the Street of the Righteous (zaddikim) in Jerusalem.

At the same time, I am disgusted by and abhor the many Poles who continue to practice their deep-rooted anti-Semitism. In helpless grief I think about the many Jews who, after they had jumped off trains or hidden in the woods, were robbed, beaten, killed or denounced and, for the price of a kilogram of bacon or sugar, turned over to the Gestapo. I also think about the Jews who were killed shortly after the war and about the pogroms organized against Jews in postwar Poland. After the bestial Nazis, this was the second worst page in history, written by Poles in Poland.

Many people of many countries supported the Nazis somewhere and somehow during that time, whether directly or indirectly, with or without intention. In the postwar years many politicians, chancellors, presidents and party and social leaders expressed their remorse and regret. On behalf of their people, they asked the victims and survivors for forgiveness.

One must wonder why no Polish politician or representative of the society or government ever considered it necessary to express regret or ask forgiveness from the Jewish victims and survivors.

With great respect and appreciation I think of the few Poles who extended their help to the Jews in those difficult times. I also understand those Poles who remained passive, fearing for themselves and their families. I can neither forget nor forgive those who helped the Germans to exterminate us. Without their collaboration, quite possibly every third or fourth Jew in Poland might have remained alive.

The way in which the Poles make use of the three million Jews killed in Poland – here, calling them Jewish victims, there, Polish martyrs of Nazism and fascism – is an insult to the dead and the living. Even the last Poles of Jewish origin, who after the war had hoped for friendship, tolerance and integrity in socialist Poland, were terribly disappointed. Voluntarily or by force, they had to leave the country. Those who still had ties to Jewish culture could lean on Judaism and be integrated into a Jewish community outside of Poland. Those who were attached to the Polish people and their culture became refugees. They often lost their own values and rarely gained any new ones. Leaving Judaism is hardly easier than being a Jew.

29 - Back in Germany

Like many others, my friend Jakob and I were completely occupied with the struggle for material gain. It was not easy to put down roots, deal with the past, and find a place to lead a normal life. It was my good fortune to have met influential people in the business world who could help me. My past in the concentration camps was never an obstacle; on the contrary, I am sure that more doors were open to me because of it. Most of the people I met received me warmly and in friendship. Some felt they had an obligation to do something for me as a sort of reparation on their part. I cannot deny that some of those people impressed me deeply with their kindness.

I had many business adventures. A special relationship which began as business and developed into a close friendship was that with Mr. A. Wilk, whom we called the "Old Man". He was a highly intelligent and interesting man who understood economics and finance well, and whose political home in the prewar years was the left. He was sure that a Jew, before the war, could belong only to the left and in the pre-Nazi era he moved in their highest circles. When the Nazis came to power in 1933 they put a price on his head but he managed to escape to France. He and his German wife were active in the French resistance and were temporarily interned. After the war he returned to East Berlin and held a high position in finance. Through one of many coincidences I became acquainted with him and a close friendship developed. He was much older than me and became like a second father.

He helped me to overcome the past and return to a normal life. He aided me and my whole family, and we owe him a lot. In the early 1950s his world became troubled. It was a time of political trials and intrigue in the east. In the ongoing show trials he knew most of the witnesses and the sentenced, and saw through everything. No wonder he felt disappointed and apathetic. From our long, intimate talks I gained an insight into those circles, which was not without effect on me.

Mr. Wilk died in the West without having turned his back on the East. He refused to accept a special grave among his comrades. Ironically, he found his eternal peace in the Jewish cemetery although his life could hardly have been called typically Jewish.

At the same time, pro-Israel activity became more common in Germany. There was fighting in Israel, illegal immigration continued, commissions and delegations came and went. I stood apart and was ashamed. My conscience tortured me, but I was not able to change my life. Occasionally I heard that other people of my age returned to school, but then just vacillated. The fear of retrogressing into misery weighed heavily upon me. A chronic anxiety about tomorrow and the future and a permanent insecurity and a feeling that I would not own tomorrow what I appreciated and possessed today was burned into my mind. This fear was not restricted to material things, but included everything I valued and worked for, including Israel and freedom.

Were all these thoughts the result of years of suffering? I do not know. We often discussed the question of whether survivors of the Holocaust had changed psychologically.

During this hard time I saw people fight for survival with their last ounce of strength, either because of their will to live or out of defiance toward their persecutors. I also saw many people collapse under the pressure of their suffering.

I developed exemplary friendships and saw how people in the depths of misery shared their last morsel of food, how they were prepared for any sacrifice. There were examples of brotherly love that grew out of empathetic pain.

But there were also people who stole food from others, regardless of previous friendships or other ties, including those between fathers and sons. Some people put a great deal of stock in the tenets of morality, while others disregarded them completely and openly. Some believed in God and their faith; other became fanatically anti-religious and rebellious. In spite of a number of exceptions, our persecutors never succeeded in replacing good human qualities with the diabolic ones they promulgated and encouraged. This is a summary of my observations and experiences, which do not necessarily refer to the functionaries of the ghettos and camps, but to the so-called gray "moor soldiers", the group to which I belonged.

Undoubtedly Majdanek and Auschwitz left their mark on all survivors. Perhaps we sometimes assume more radical and extreme positions because of our experiences. We tended to become less tolerant and more easily unnerved than before.

During the years of captivity and slavery, we learned to appreciate freedom and independence. It seems to me that the anxieties of the past always hang over us like the sword of Damocles. No promises, protests or resolutions from political parties, governments or nations were sufficient to free us from this Auschwitz complex. We learned to mistrust in that camp; I confess, however, that as to Jewish existence and survival, I trust Israel and Israel only.

Many of my friends traveled legally or illegally to Israel. Again I felt put to the test and fought yet another battle with my conscience in order to arrive at the right decision. In accordance with my convictions, I should have gone to Israel, perhaps even to a kibbutz, but I did not go. I was far removed from life in a kibbutz and felt more attracted to individuality and close family life; I had experienced more than enough of group living. I also did not feel that I was in a position to fight again, as the years 1945-46 would have demanded of us. Tired and battered, I felt that I had contributed my share of suffering. Like Adam and Eve with the apple, I was corrupted. I was convinced then and still am that I was not faithful to my belief and was therefore wrong. I admit that I followed the easier path of complacency and egotism, but I am not trying to justify my actions. I accept responsibility and have since lived with a guilty conscience. If I had gone to Israel immediately after the liberation I probably would have become a good Israeli and an ardent Zionist. But this can be said of so many others as well.

My wife was also reared in a Zionist home, and was attracted to Israel and life in a kibbutz. It took many discussions and disputes before we finally reached a mutually satisfactory decision. We were married in Marburg in 1946 and lived there for some time in a small, rented attic apartment. Our landlady was a decent, religious and elderly woman with whom we got along very well. She had never known Jews before; after she found out that we had no horns or claws, she was very happy with us. One day she declared that if Jews were ever persecuted again, she would certainly hide us. We could count on that.

Feelings of guilt and the urge to atone are evidently shared by a large number of the German people. As a Jew one can see this as a positive step. Nevertheless, we feel uneasy around such people. Unfortunately, it seems natural for some, even if they are not anti-Semites, to assume that persecution of Jews can happen again, even after Auschwitz. The example of our landlady in Marburg is stuck in my mind, because it is so typical of the many people who either want to strangle us out of hate, or smother us with brotherly love. We would be content to be allowed to live as human beings and as a people like any other, without ever again needing to rely on others.

30 - The Big Disappointment

Like everyone at this time I started at zero without any special training. The will and desire for a more secure life was my only starting capital. My experiences were the substitute for my lack of knowledge. I built, relied and counted on the people I trusted, and was lucky to get paid back threefold. It was with deep satisfaction that I noted and appreciated that I was at last on the sunny side. Time was good to me in every respect after those terrible years. I somehow felt compensated for my previous suffering. The rewards were family happiness, luck and business and social success, which I enjoyed sharing with my friends. At this time I also got closer to my brother-in-law K. Zweigel, from whom I learned a great deal. We developed a warm friendship that lasts to this day.

For my friend and camp brother Jakob with whom I lived, the world looked different at this time. Unfortunately he was always weak and sick, tied down to house and bed, and consequently without any initiative. I, on the other hand, remained relatively healthy, restless and was always on the road. We lived together and shared everything including money and business success. There was no limit to what I did in order to strengthen him physically and morally. As it turned out, it was an ideal friendship, free of jealousy, malice and rivalry. Each of us – if not entirely satisfied with himself – was surely proud of the other. In our circle we were envied.

For almost twenty years the relationship flourished in perfect harmony. But after so many years as fate would have it, my friend Jakob succeeded to occupy the driver's seat. He turned against me. Betraying my trust, he denounced our friendship and dictated terribly unfair terms and conditions. I was shocked and overwhelmed. This was the greatest disappointment of my life and is to this day. I was sick, heartbroken and suffered interminably. Too late I realized that I had underestimated Jakob and his inordinate desire to flex his muscles and bask in the limelight at any cost.

In the following years my problems multiplied beyond my control. For the first time in my life I couldn't manage my own affairs. I was ashamed and at my lowest point. What I was left with was justice, righteousness, and a very clean conscience. This gave me the strength to overcome, but not to forget.

31 - Three Dates

In my new life, three dates were of great significance.

April 15, 1945

This was the day of the liberation and the birth of a new life in freedom. The greatest genocide in history was over and 40% of the Jewish people had been exterminated. Auschwitz, Majdanek and Treblinka, synonymous with terror, ceased to exist. It was a great day for a simple Jew like me whom the murderers had forgotten to kill.

On that day I remembered my parents, my family, my relatives and all those who were unable to experience the liberation.

The feeling of being a victim and a witness to the most heinous crime in human history tortured and depressed me. To withhold relating my experiences was for me an injustice to mankind. To relive it in the telling was, however, exceedingly difficult.

Even today, after forty years, the veil of Auschwitz has not been lifted. Everything that is Jewish or relates to Israel or to fear, terror, danger and persecution is tied to that veil, even if Auschwitz as it was then does not exist anymore. The symbolic Auschwitz has remained, however, as a symbol for genocide, pain and inhumanity, especially against Jews.

November 29, 1947

On that day the United Nations (UN) decided by a large majority to allow the foundation of the State of Israel. It was the day of the world's conscience. For people with my past, it brought a renewal of faith and confidence, and it was also a day of gratitude to mankind. With the founding of the State of Israel, I believed that the conscience of the world had finally been awakened to the outrageous injustices of Auschwitz. People finally realized that it is impossible and unreasonable for Jews to always exist as a minority, always dependent on the mercy and goodwill of other nations.

Today, only forty years later, people have grown tired of their Auschwitz debts. They have become more interested in pools of oil than in the pools of blood in the concentration camps.

Unfortunately, there are many indications that the UN is again looking for a Jewish scapegoat. Lies and fanaticism, symptomatic of Auschwitz, are on the increase within that body. But we Jews should have learned one lesson from ancient and recent history, namely never to rely on the world and its conscience, politicians, parties and religions. Never again should we rely on others. Never again should we become defenseless and dependent.

May 15, 1948

The State of Israel was founded. It was the greatest day for the Jewish people in the last two thousand years. In the joy engendered by this revolutionary and long-awaited event, even the pains of the recent past faded.

A Holocaust survivor should not regard the founding of Israel as compensation for the victims of the Nazi regime. Our tears on that day were for the six million victims who were not allowed to experience the glorious event. But we did unconsciously regard this achievement as a small consolation for our pain and sacrifices.

It was a day on which the dream of centuries finally became a reality, a day on which the Jewish people again were able to put their fate into their own hands. Two thousand years of wandering and oppression, of persecution and contempt, of always suffering as a minority without home and country, were finally over. On that day we became the equal of all other nations and peoples. We were unified in the belief and conviction that only a state of our own could prevent a repetition of Auschwitz and the Holocaust. I have added to my Jewish creed the belief that the existence of a Jewish state is a precondition for the existence of a Jewish people. With the Auschwitz number on my arm, the fact was tattooed into my mind that Auschwitz was exclusively created for us Jews and that not one single cohesive body of people wanted to fight against it. Since then and because of this state, Auschwitz will never be repeated.

By means of the written description of those terrible years as I and my fellow sufferers experienced them, I think that I have fulfilled an obligation to the Jewish men, women and children who were killed by the Nazis and their abettors.

I feel somewhat relieved, but I do not know whether I shall find more peace.

Even today I still cannot accept the one big injustice: why? Why did we Jews have to suffer so much, so much more, than other peoples and nations? Why were we – just because we were born as Jews – forced by other men to suffer and die? Why?

32 - In Memory of My Hevra

It was my special wish to mention, with fondness, my Hevra with whom I spent my early childhood and with whom I grew up. After the loss of our families, we grew together into a unique, close-knit family. We were so intimate and so devoted that each of us was prepared to sacrifice his or her life for the other. This mutual love and loyalty became the very core of our lives. In the years of misery this friendship solidified, proved and confirmed itself. The quote from the Bible, "love your friends as you love yourself," was realized completely among our Hevra.

The spirit of self-sacrifice in our group – of thirteen boys and girls – was the highlight of our otherwise drab, young lives. But, alas, all of them died. With their youth and potential, they joined the six million victims of the Holocaust. With their resistance against the Nazi killers, their noble and humane way of life, their Jewish, Zionist ideals and their dedication and comradery, they have earned their exalted place in Jewish history.

As the only survivor of my Hevra, I regard it as my sacred task and obligation to write this epitaph for them and to erect a monument to their memory with this book.

Glossary of Foreign Words

Aharit-hayamim – "The End of Days" (biblical concept).

A.K. (Armja Krajowa) – Polish resistance group led from London.

Al hatoim shehatanu – "For the sins we committed".

Al heit – "For the sin".

Bar Kochba – Leader of the last big rebellion of the Jews against Rome.

Ben Torah – Torah scholar.

Bimber – Homemade vodka made from grain, potatoes or turnips.

Brit Mila – Circumcision and name-giving on the eight day after birth.

Daffke – "Defiance".

Dybbuk – The ghost of the dead in the body of a living person. Jewish drama by Anski.

Ein breira – "No escape".

El-moleh-rahamim – "God of Mercy".

Gemara – "The completion", i.e. completion and discussion of the Mishnah.

Hanukah – Festival of lights in memory of the Maccabees.

Hashomer-Hatzair – Jewish Zionist youth organization.

Hereg ve-heneq – "Killing and strangling".

Heshbon-banefesh – "Soul-searching".

Hevra – "Circle of friends".

Josche Kalb – Jewish play by Singer.

Kaddish – Prayer for the dead.

Keren-Kayemet – Jewish Zionist fund.

Kibbutz – Collective form of life in Israel.

Kosher – In the context used: "legal".

Leshana habayha b'Yerushalaim – "Next year in Jerusalem", a prayer on Yom Kippur.

Maccabees – Jewish heroes of the rebellion against the Greeks in 160 B.C.

Mikva – Ritual bath.

Mi-lamovel – "Who is to die?"

Mi-lehaim – "Who is to live?"

Moshe Bauer – Nickname for a stupid, brutal man.

Pesah – Passover. Jewish holiday commemorating the Exodus on which no leavened bread is eaten.

Purim – Jewish celebration of the liberation of the Jews from Hamman in Persia.

Schmalzowniks – Polish bounty hunters who turned Jews over to the Gestapo.

Shliah Zibur – "Messenger of the Congregation", prayer leader.

Shma Israel – "Hear, O Israel", Jewish prayer.

Sqila, srefa – "Stoning, burning".

Stadlanut – Mediation, persuasion by supplication and influence.

Tallit – Prayer shawl.

Tarbut School – Hebrew-Zionist school.

Tefilin – Phylacteries.

Tisha-beav – Day of mourning and fasting for the destruction of the Temple.

Tralala – Code word for jumping off trains.

Trefa – In the context used: "illegal".

Tzores – Trouble, suffering.

*Yom Kipp*ur – Day of Atonement, holiday of fasting.

Zeena-Reena – "Go and See" "translation" (actually paraphrase) of the Torah in Yiddish.

About the Author

"After the Great Tragedy, my strongest wish for everyone was for a secure State of Israel; for myself I yearned for a family and a tranquil life."

"I have the good fortune to have a happy family. We have two sons and grandchildren, and we have all remained faithful to Judaism and its traditions."

"In all these years, I have, for the most part, been successfully employed. Nevertheless, my life has remained profoundly influenced by the past."

"Whatever transpires in this world I perceive through the mirror of the past."

Joseph Schupack (1922-1989)

Further Reading

Amsterdam Publishers Holocaust Memoirs:

Outcry - Holocaust Memoirs. A brutally honest survivor story of human endurance in WW2, by Manny Steinberg is available as paperback (ISBN 13: 978-9082103137) and as Kindle eBook.

This bestselling memoir has been published in English, French, Chinese and Czech. German and Spanish editions forthcoming.

Hank Brodt Holocaust Memoirs − A Candle and a Promise by Deborah Donnelly is available as paperback (ISBN 13: 978-1537653488) and as Kindle eBook.

The Mission of Abbé Glasberg in the French Resistance during WWII by Lucien Lazare is available as paperback (ISBN 13: 978-1522840954) and as Kindle eBook.

Colophon

Title: The Dead Years - Holocaust Memoirs

Author: Joseph Schupack

ISBN13: 978-9492371164

ISBN10: 949-2371162

Copyright text © Mark Shupac and Joel Shupac

Publisher: Amsterdam Publishers, The Netherlands

info@amsterdampublishers.com

Fully edited and revised edition, 2017

Originally published in German as: *Tote Jahre, Eine jüdische Leidensgeschichte*, Tübingen (Katzmann), 1984.